"Steve Sax has had both the highs and lows that can result in great substance and multiple achievements. His book, *SHIFT: Change Your Mindset and You Change Your World*, reflects the wisdom he has gained through his experiences. It's a terrific and motivating read—and Steve is a true winner."

DONALD TRUMP

SHIFT

Heather,

Success is a choice!

Steve Sax

SHIFT

CHANGE YOUR **MINDSET**

and you

CHANGE YOUR **WORLD**

STEVE SAX

Published by Advantage, Charleston, South Carolina.
Member of Advantage Media Group.

ADVANTAGE is a registered trademark and the Advantage colophon is a trademark of Advantage Media Group, Inc.

Printed in the United States of America.

ISBN: 978-1-59932-223-0
LCCN: 2010917661

This publication is designed to provide accurate and authoritative information in regard to the subject matter covered. It is sold with the understanding that the publisher is not engaged in rendering legal, accounting, or other professional services. If legal advice or other expert assistance is required, the services of a competent professional person should be sought.

Advantage Media Group is proud to be a part of the Tree Neutral™ program. Tree Neutral offsets the number of trees consumed in the production and printing of this book by taking proactive steps such as planting trees in direct proportion to the number of trees used to print books. To learn more about Tree Neutral, please visit **www.treeneutral.com**. To learn more about Advantage's commitment to being a responsible steward of the environment, please visit **www.advantagefamily.com/green**

Advantage Media Group is a leading publisher of business, motivation, and self-help authors. Do you have a manuscript or book idea that you would like to have considered for publication? Please visit **www.amgbook.com** or call **1.866.775.1696**

To my Parents, John and Nancy

Who gave me their fabric of life...

And the attention to stick by me,

And the need to stick it to me,

And set this path for me...

Until we meet again, I remain,

Your Most Affectionate Son,

STEPHEN

TABLE OF CONTENTS

TABLE OF CONTENTS

MAKING THE SHIFT

'm sure you've read a lot of motivational books that promise to tell you the secret of easy success. These books always claim that right after you finish reading them you'll immediately start a successful new business or move right into the corner office. Well, we've all been around long enough to know that there's no quick and easy route to achieving your goals in business and in life. Yes, you need to dream big, but you also need to recognize that there's no such thing as an overnight success.

I'm not saying you can't start your own business or get the promotion you desire. In fact, I know you can. The only catch is that there's no such thing as overnight success. Achievement only comes through planning, practice and hard work, but all that sweat, sacrifice and elbow grease you expend is the reason your success will be so rewarding.

When I hear people wish for overnight success, I think about Muhammad Ali beating Sonny Liston for the heavyweight boxing title in Miami in 1964. Ali shocked the entire sporting world when he beat the heavily favored Liston. Nobody thought Ali could do it. Liston had knocked out the previous champion, Floyd Patterson, in the first round just two years before. Yet Ali beat Liston in six rounds. That's only 18 minutes in the ring. Suddenly Ali was the heavyweight champion and the most famous athlete on the planet. After the fight, some wiseacre said to Ali, "Not bad for a night's work, eh?"

A night's work? Not exactly. Ali answered that he didn't win the fight that night. Winning the fight was the result of his hard work and preparation. "I won this fight three months ago when I decided to train and beat this man," Ali said. "I won this fight in the gym three months ago."

The truth is that success is built on a series of small conquests that over time build up momentum and take on a life of their own. Success is not about one grandiose event; it's about shifting your mindset so that you're pretty good every day and create a wave of positivity that makes success a habit, as natural and unstoppable a force as inertia.

Let's talk about inertia. It is one of Sir Isaac Newton's laws of motion. The law of inertia states that an object in motion remains in motion until it is interrupted by an outside force and that an object at rest will remain at rest until it is started into motion by an outside force. The same principle applies to achieving success. You are the outside force. You create the momentum of your life's journey. If you want to move forward, you'll move forward. If you want to remain in the same place, that's where you'll stay. The only force that can stop your momentum is yourself. In other words, if you keep doing what you're doing, you'll keep getting what you're getting.

Imagine your life is a blank canvas and that you are a painter. You need to start painting something positive and creative on that canvas every day, no matter how small it is. You're going to find that when you make all those positive strokes with your paintbrush, the canvas will begin to take on a life of its own. Every little thing we do affects whether we will accomplish our goals in life. With every positive act, you're putting pennies in the bank of success—pennies of confidence, pennies of self-esteem, pennies of positivity. When you put those pennies of positive energy and good-natured feelings into the bank of success every day, over time you're going to build yourself a fortune, both professionally and personally.

STEVE'S TIP

How do you start creating something positive every day? Each morning write down a list of everything you want to do that day to help you stay on track and create something positive. Write down the task you have to do and when you'll do it, and then the next task, and the next, so you know what you're doing the entire day.

It's extremely important to stay on task, so make sure you complete those tasks on your list when you say you will. Don't say, "This can wait for tomorrow." Do it today, so that tomorrow you can take your next small step toward your goals. In addition to the lists I make every day, I also make a list of what I want to accomplish at the beginning of every year. I ask myself: "What do I want to accomplish by the end of the first quarter of the year, by the halfway point, by the end of the third quarter, and finally at the end of the year?" Make lists for both your professional development—what you want to achieve at work and in your career—and your goals for your personal life—what you want to achieve as a parent, a spouse and a friend. Making lists of your goals both daily and long-term is one of the most important steps you can take toward achieving success. Those positive things you keep in your head are only good intentions, but once you write them down, they become tasks you can complete.

The key to realizing your goals in life is to shift your mindset away from immediate gratification and toward the long process of building something of value that lasts. If you're committed and you work hard, you will achieve success, but your journey won't be a line going straight up in the air. You're not going to rocket to the top like a hit record. Anyone who tells you that is selling you an empty promise, because it's impossible to achieve anything of real value without hard work and sacrifice. On the road to success, you're going to have times when you doubt yourself and times when people will question whether you're doing the right thing. You'll have setbacks. You're even going to have times where that line is going to go down, but when you shift your outlook and create something positive every day, over time that line of success will keep climbing up at a 45-degree angle.

It's like the stock market. When you follow the market, you know not to overreact to the daily ups and downs of a particular stock you own. What you're looking for is long-term performance. You should approach your goals in life the same way. You'll have ups and down every day and every week, but if your mindset is to create something positive every day, you'll see movement steadily toward your goals over time, just as a successful stock increases in value over time despite the daily blips of the market.

STEVE'S TIP

People who work in the stock market know that you can't get caught up in daily fluctuations or hiccups. The same thing goes on in our lives, whether at work or home. Don't overreact to the daily dramas and quasi-emergencies. Instead, stay focused on your long-term goals.

One thing I can tell you for certain is that you will face obstacles and difficulties as you work toward accomplishing your goals in life. The important thing to realize is that those setbacks often are the times that strengthen your character and help you prosper in the long run. Adversity has a way of introducing you to yourself, as I know firsthand.

I had a successful baseball career with the Los Angeles Dodgers, New York Yankees, Chicago White Sox and Oakland Athletics. I won two World Series rings and made five all-star teams, but in my second season in the big leagues I developed a throwing problem, which threatened everything I had worked so hard for.

I got drafted into baseball by Dodgers scout Ronnie King in the ninth round of the 1978 draft, and Ronnie always told me that one of the main reasons he drafted me was because I had an exceptional throwing arm.

Well, early in my second season I made an error in one of the first games. It wasn't a simple misplayed ball or poor throw to first. I'd thrown a ball from the outfield on a relay play back to home plate, and the ball ricocheted off of catcher Mike Scioscia's shin guard and went to the backstop and the run scored. I didn't necessarily have to throw the ball on this particular play because the runner at third had stopped, but I went ahead and hummed the ball in toward home plate and the ball ricocheted off the catcher's shin guard and my error allowed the runner to score.

It was the kind of thing that could happen to anyone, but I started thinking about this error way too much. It really got in my head. Then I looked in the newspaper and saw that I had made a couple errors early in the season. I started to think, "Wow, I'm on pace to make 100-and-something errors this year." So I began to place all this horrible pressure on myself, and of course I made a throwing error the next day. Then I made a couple more throwing errors later on in the week. Pretty soon I had this horrible monster in my head that I couldn't get rid of.

The monster of negative thoughts just got so big that I couldn't overcome it. I was going to bed with it. I was waking up with it. Sleeping with it. Pretty soon it just got to be something I couldn't control anymore. And then finally it got to the point where I had to admit to myself that I had a huge problem, and I had to get over it.

After a couple of months of regularly making throwing errors, I was sure that my career was in jeopardy. The more I worked at my throwing problem, the worse it got. Conventional wisdom tells us that if we work at something hard enough we get over it, but that wasn't the case for me. The team and I tried everything. The Dodger brass would bring me out to second base at Dodger Stadium in the middle of the afternoon when nobody was there, blindfold me, and have me throw the ball to first base. I'd throw it to first base without an error every single time blindfolded, but I just couldn't make the throw in the game.

My low point as a ballplayer was when I made a humongous error against the San Diego Padres on a beautiful late spring day. It was the most perfect setting for a baseball game you could imagine, something that Norman Rockwell would have painted. There were 60,000 people watching the game in San Diego and we were winning. And they hit one to me and I threw the ball away late in the game and we lost. That was the low point for me. I just couldn't take it anymore. It got too heavy. After the third out, I ran up to the clubhouse, threw my glove in my locker, and I just screamed it out: "Man, I can't take anymore. If this is the last thing I do in my sports career, I am going to beat this throwing problem, and I do not care what it takes. I don't care. I will come within an inch of sacrificing my own soul. I will give up everything I have before I give up. I will burn every bridge I've ever had in this world to beat this." I was tired of being controlled. I was tired of being manipulated. I felt like I was being violated. It was time to plant my flag and summon all my inner resources.

That's when my dad talked to me. You need to understand that my dad was larger than life. He was the strongest man I ever saw. And he was tough. He made John Wayne look like a wimp. When I was a kid, I saw him in a fight once— someone had flipped him off—and I knew no matter how big I got I would never want to mess with him.

A German immigrant, my dad was a truck driver and a farmer in Sacramento. He was the kind of guy who never said "I love you," never said "I'm sorry." He was born and raised during the Depression and that's how men were back then. He wasn't a big talker, he was a doer. My dad was never going to star in "Laughs Unlimited" or write a romance novel. That's just the way he was with us kids. (However, he was extremely affectionate with my mother and thought she was the greatest thing to ever walk on earth.)

My dad was a darn good ballplayer too. When he played American Legion ball, he beat out Woodie Held for shortstop and Held ended up playing 15 seasons in the major leagues. Needless to say, my dad was my hero, the greatest man I ever knew.

Unfortunately, my dad also suffered heart problems. Not that he ever complained about it. I remember once talking with my dad while he was laying in bed right before having open-heart surgery. He was about to undergo serious surgery and he was relaxed and talking with me like it was just a normal day. I once saw him crawl from the garage through the kitchen and into the bathroom to relieve himself of a slipped disc by laying in a hot tub. He never asked for anyone's help, and he never said his back hurt, that's just the way he was.

About a week after the Padres game, I called home to talk to my dad. I couldn't get my mind off my throwing problem—it was like a bad piece of luggage that never went anywhere—and so gradually every conversation I had always led to that issue. I told my dad how desperate I was to beat this problem, and how fixing my throwing problem wasn't about sports anymore; it was a personal quest.

My dad said, "Listen, I'm going to tell you something. One day you're going to wake up and the problem is going to be gone. I know because I went through this same problem when I played baseball in high school and it can happen to anybody."

When my dad said that, I understood that if this same problem could happen to somebody as formidable as my dad, someone who is that big and ominous, then maybe I'm not so weird. Maybe I'm not so strange. If the same throwing problem happened to my dad—the biggest, strongest man in the world—then it could happen to anybody.

What my dad was telling me was that even the strongest people aren't immune to adversity. To get your confidence back, he said, you have to face the thing that's bothering you and you have to bite it right in the face. If you fight it a little bit at a time every day, pretty soon the problem will be gone. That meant everything to me, because I wasn't hopeless anymore. I could see myself overcoming this obstacle because my dad had faced down the same problem.

My dad was absolutely right because I started getting my confidence back little by little, and pretty soon the throwing problem dissipated. After a while, it just disappeared. I took extra grounders every day and I started feeling so confident in my abilities again that I couldn't wait for them to hit me the ball. I finished the final 34 games of the year without an error, and I signed my first big major league contract when the season was over. I had conquered this thing, and I was able to do it in large part because of what my father had told me that day on the phone.

THE LESSON

Great leaders are great storytellers. When you can tell someone a story that relates to his or her own situation, then you can change the way they feel about themselves. That's what successful leaders do. I can't recount verbatim what my dad said to me that day, but I'll never forget how he made me feel. He made me feel like I could conquer this terrible problem. He gave me belief in myself. When you lead people, always remember that the most important thing you can do is improve the way they feel, and stories are a great way to accomplish this.

That night after I spoke to my father, the team flew to Cincinnati. I remember getting to bed at a hotel at quarter till 3 in the morning and I got a call at about quarter till 6 in the morning. It was my manager, Tommy Lasorda, and he told me I had to come to his room.

This was during the worst period of my throwing errors, and I thought, "Oh my God, they've traded me or, even worse, I've been sent down to Triple A."

When I went to the elevator and pushed the button, the door opened and I saw my brother David in the elevator. My brother was also on the team, and Tommy had obviously called him first. We both looked at each other and said, "It's Dad." We knew it. When we were in rookie ball in 1978 we had to go home because my dad had had a heart attack. So this was something that we had seen before. We got to Tommy's room, and he was in there crying. I'll never forget what he said to David and me.

"As a manager, this is the hardest thing I've ever had to do," Tommy said. "But I have to tell you boys that you lost your father."

I don't think that my dad knew that he was going to die on that day he talked to me on the phone, but he knew that he wasn't going to be here forever. He was only 47 years old, but in that time he did so much for his children and for my mother. And his final gift to me helped me save my baseball career. It also helped me become a better businessman, a better father, and a better man.

The whole concept of *Shift: Change Your Mindset and You Change Your World* started that afternoon when I talked to my father and today it's still the backbone of how I plan for success. This book will show you how you can realize your goals and dreams through the six elements that will help you create lasting prosperity in business and in life: motivation, empowerment, attitude, humility, leadership and perseverance. So let's get started.

CHAPTER 1

MOTIVATION

HOW BIG IS YOUR WHY?

The best advice I can give you about motivation is to dream big. Dream so big that it might even be unimaginable because some of the greatest innovations the world has ever seen began as the wildest of dreams. The first thing you need to do is to find what your passion center is. You have to know what it is that you love to do. You have to find your passion because when you are passionate about something, chances are you're going to be really good at it.

Think about it. The best salespeople are passionate about their product. The best financial analysts are passionate about creating wealth. The best doctors are passionate about healing illnesses. Even people who like to burglarize homes. They're criminals, but they love being criminals. It's too bad, but frankly they're pretty good at it. To achieve something that is significant and lasting, you need to have a burning desire to achieve your goal. That's your "why." And if it is big enough, then the "how-to" doesn't matter.

When you have a burning desire to achieve something, you're willing to burn every bridge behind you, you're willing to take a chance, and you're willing to put it all on the table, roll the dice and say, "I don't care what the consequences are." When I was playing baseball, and when I started my business career afterward, I didn't care what the consequences were. I was willing to fail. That's when you know your "why" is big enough, when you're not afraid to fail. You essentially need to surrender to the outcome.

STEVE'S TIP

How do you know when your "why" is big enough? You'll know that your desire is strong enough to succeed if you're willing to pay the price and if you're willing to sacrifice. When I talk to people about motivation and success, I hear so many excuses that I just tell people to number them. No. 1, "I got called into work." No. 2, "My car blew up." No. 3, "I'm a little tired." No. 4, "My wife won't let me." No. 5, "The kids are keeping me too busy." The deal is that if your why is big enough then all those excuses just don't matter. If you can think of all these reasons that prevent you from accomplishing something that you say is important, then your desire just isn't strong enough. In other words, you don't want it enough. You have to do a gut check. After your gut check, if you continue to find reasons why you can't do something, then your "why" is just not big enough.

The phrase "burning desire" actually comes from an ancient military campaign. In 711 AD, the Muslim general Tariq ibn Ziyad led his men to Gibraltar. As his army assembled for the coming battle, Ziyad asked the men to look back at the ships that brought them across the sea. Ziyad had ordered the ships to be set afire. When Ziyad's men saw those ships burning, they knew that retreat was impossible and their only option was to fight and to win, which they did against the odds. That's the kind of desire you want to have because the road to success is never an easy journey and you'll need courage, grit and determination to achieve your dreams.

You can look at the risk of failure one of two ways. Some people say, "I think I'd like to accomplish this goal, but I might fail at it so I probably shouldn't try." I saw people in professional sports that were like that too. But you will have a better chance of success if you treat risks as opportunities rather than chances to fail. That's the difference between somebody who is going to put it all out on the line and somebody who is going to hold back and be a little bit timid because he or she is afraid to fail.

Do you know the story of Edwin C. Barnes? He was born back in 1877 in Wisconsin. He was certainly not born into the aristocracy. Barnes wasn't a man of great means, and he wasn't a man of superior intelligence. You might call him just a regular dude.

As Napoleon Hill wrote in his Depression-era classic, *Think and Grow Rich*, Barnes had a big dream. He decided he wanted to become a partner of—not work for, but work with—the greatest inventor of his time, Thomas Edison.

So Barnes boarded a train in Wisconsin and arrived at the Edison's offices in East Orange, N.J., in 1905. He didn't have the money for a train ticket so he rode what they called "blind baggage." That means Barnes was basically a hobo who rode a rickety old train car from Wisconsin to New Jersey because it was the only way he could afford to travel. When he arrived at Edison's offices, Barnes announced himself and then asked Edison for a job.

Let's put this story in today's terms. This is equivalent to somebody boarding a train in Wisconsin and traveling all the way to Seattle, then showing up at the Microsoft campus and saying to Bill Gates, "Hi, Bill. I'm here to be your new partner."

Crazy, right? Well, that's what Barnes did, and the crazier thing is that it worked. Not right away, of course. After Barnes introduced himself, Edison looked at him and thought, "Hmm, this is your average tramp." After traveling from Wisconsin in a train car, Barnes looked and even smelled the part. Still, Edison hired him right on the spot. Not to work in the capacity that Barnes wanted. Edison didn't hire this unusual job seeker as his partner. He hired him as a gopher. You know, "Barnes, I need you to clean the floor," "Barnes, go get lunch for everybody," and "Hey Barnes, I need a coffee." That was the kind of job Barnes had at Edison's offices.

However, Barnes didn't complain that he was stuck in a dead-end job. He saw this position as a great opportunity. Barnes was not looking for a job; he was looking for an opportunity. There's a difference. Barnes wanted to do something special in his life and he needed an opportunity to show Edison what he could do. That meant he would be on time. He would work hard. He would be respectful in the workplace. He would work when he was sick and he didn't feel like coming into the office. In short, Barnes was going to show Edison that he possessed all of the traits it took to be successful.

For five years, Barnes swept the floor and got the lunches and made the coffee. Think about what he didn't do. He didn't say, "You know what? I came here to work as a partner with Edison. I'm not sweeping the floor. I'm going to go down the street, and I'm going to get a real sales job for a company that appreciates me." He also didn't say, "Thomas Edison is in the other room; the greatest inventor who ever lived. What the heck am I doing here? This is a hare-brained idea, and I should spank myself for even thinking this big. I'm going back to Wisconsin."

Instead, Barnes waited because he knew that opportunities come in unexpected ways, from unusual angles and through side doors. He just needed to be in the right position to take advantage when these opportunities came. Barnes got his chance when Edison invented the Ediphone, a very crude, large and cumbersome precursor to the tape recorder.

Remember, this was 1905. We didn't have a thriving and bustling technology-based economy. It wasn't even the roaring '20s yet. In 1905, people were just looking to put some bread and food on the table, not to buy a tape recorder. Most of them probably wouldn't even know what a tape recorder was; forget about knowing what to do with one. So Edison's salespeople said, "This will never work. We're in a tough time and people aren't going to buy a bulky and expensive luxury object."

Edison disagreed. He thought the Ediphone was a good product with a bright future. He was looking for someone to raise his hand and become the leader of selling this product. Guess who raised his hand? It was the floor sweeper; the guy who rode the rickety train thousands of miles to get a chance and an opportunity to work with the greatest inventor alive. The guy who had no business being there, Edwin Barnes raised his hand. And so you know what Edison did? He gave Barnes a chance.

Barnes told Edison, "Not only will I sell the Ediphone, I'll sell it more on a regional level but I'll blow it out of the water on a national level." And that's exactly what Barnes did. Not long afterward, people started saying, "Invented by Edison, installed by Barnes." Barnes had become partners with the greatest inventor of his time because he did not quit. He did not give up on his dream. He hung in there until he got his opportunity and when that opportunity finally came he made the most of it.

In later years, Edison said that he could not describe the look on the face of Barnes when Barnes first walked into his office all those years ago, but Edison did say, "I could see that the man was not going to give up until he got what he came for."

THE LESSON

Thomas Edison made an investment in a human being. He took a chance on a guy who looked like a bum, a guy who didn't have anything except a will to succeed. However, Edwin Barnes is one of the best examples of how you need to forget about failure and give everything you have to your goals if you're going to succeed. Barnes put his family and everything that was near and dear to him on the line. All Edison and Barnes had in common was the will to succeed and the wherewithal to take a chance, and together they created one of the greatest partnerships in the history of business.

When I think of burning desire, I think of Edwin Barnes. If Barnes' desire was weak, he wouldn't have become Edison's partner. He would have returned home to Wisconsin with his tail between his legs (if he ever got on that train to New Jersey in the first place). A small fire gives off a small amount of heat. That's how it works in nature and that's how it goes with desire as well. If your desire doesn't burn inside you, if you can't feel its heat, it won't be strong enough to get you through the learning curve of any new skill set. That is why we always revert back to our passion center. You have to find out what your passion is. Forget everything else. Forget about what it's going to take to get there. Forget about the money involved. Forget about all of that. It doesn't matter. You have to start with what's going to be the root of your success, and that's going to be what your passion is.

I believe that whatever you focus on the most in your mind, whatever you concentrate on the most is going to grow the most, so you need to put the focus on something you love, not harp on something that bothers you. I harped on my throwing problem and that's why it got worse. I woke up with it every day. I thought about it every minute. I couldn't eat without thinking about it. I would wake up with it, and go to bed with it. It was all I thought about, and look how horrible that got.

Your mindset works a little bit like peer pressure and how the attitudes of the people around you affect your attitude. When people hear the words "peer pressure," they think, "Oh my God, that's horrible, that peer pressure stuff." And peer pressure can be a pretty negative thing if you're around the wrong kind of people. But if you're around the right kind of people, peer pressure is a great thing.

If you're around positive people in your life who are determined to succeed and live according to core values, than peer pressure can be a tremendously advantageous element in your life. It just depends on whom you're around and the people you hang out with. Your friends are important in determining your mindset. We start to meld into the type of surroundings that we're in, and if you don't like your surroundings, then you may need to change them.

People who like to grumble about their jobs and really don't get anywhere in their life have a tendency to flock together. And people who are successful spend their time with other successful people because they have the same things in common, they have the same things to talk about, and they have the same goals. The same thing happens with what we think about in our minds. If we have negative thoughts going in our minds, those things are going to grow into a big form of negativity. If we have positive thoughts and if we have good things that we think about, those are going to become big successes. One of the things I like to say is, "Dream big. Dream silly, man. Dream as big as you possibly can. Dream about great things that happen."

STEVE'S TIP

We talk a lot about the power of the individual, but your peers exert a great deal of influence on you and your goals, so it's important to surround yourself with people who share the same dreams and ambitions.

I want you to do a little exercise. Whatever your dream is, I want you to imagine that goal or dream is in a box. Look at the box and say, "OK, I have a desire to do something and if I put my heart and mind into it, I know it's going to take me three-to-five years to conquer this thing, but at the end of that time, I get what's in the box. When you open up the box, is that dream everything that you wanted it to be? Is it worth it? You have to ask yourself, "What is your why?" Because if your "why" is big enough, the how-to doesn't matter.

Let's say that you start from point zero and it takes you five years. You know what I call the stuff in the middle? All that sacrifice and labor, and all the dedication and the long hours, and standing up to the naysayers. That's all minutiae. I had the same things happen to me. Barnes went through the same thing when he was taking all those lunch orders and sweeping all those floors. It's the small stuff and you shouldn't sweat it. If your dream is big enough, and your passion is strong enough, those obstacles don't mean a darned thing.

SHIFT

One of my high school coaches told me not to sign with the Dodgers because he thought I was never going to make it in the big leagues. He said I was not developed enough yet. "You have a full ride to Arizona," he said. "Why don't you just play it safe and see what happens after college?"

I was 5'11", close to 6 feet, but I weighed only 160 pounds, and I didn't really grow until well into my senior year. This coach wasn't a bad guy. He was just looking at it like, "This kid's not big enough. They're going to break the bat in his hand if he goes out and faces these big pitchers." He told me I was not ready, but he couldn't X-ray my chest. He couldn't see the size of my heart and what I had burning inside. I didn't listen to him and signed with the Dodgers, and three years and two months after he told me that, I was wearing a Dodgers uniform and playing in the World Series against the Yankees at Yankee Stadium. That coach didn't know how big my "why" was.

When I travel and speak to people around the country, I meet a lot of people out there who feel a bit displaced and who are really unhappy with their life situation. Sometimes we get mired in the muck of work and feel like we're just going by to get by and just kind of stumbling through things. It happens sometimes. We get stuck in ruts and lose track of our goals.

If that sounds like you, I want you to take a bold step in your life. Ask yourself if you like your personal situation, and if you're not happy and not living life to the fullest, you need to step out and make a change, and go for something that makes you happy. Because life isn't worth going through just to muddle through it. Get into that passion center. Ask yourself what you really love to do. If you can answer that, then you can find what you really want to do in your life.

That's the first and most important step you can take on the road to success. Because I've got some news for you: it's not going to be an easy ride. Success takes hard work. You've got to be tough, and if you're working from your passion center you'll have the strength and the verve to overcome the obstacles and adversity that will come your way.

I've had to make some bold changes in my life before, but I did it. Sometimes there's no reward unless you roll the dice, especially in today's challenging economy, where you really need to take the initiative to get ahead. Don't be timid about your future. Risk takers are the people who are successful in the world today.

THE LESSON

If your why is big enough, follow it anywhere. I'm a strong believer in college, I think it's great, but if somebody tells me that his or her desire is so big that he or she is willing to put it all on the line and doesn't care what the ramifications are, and if I see that he or she has a heart that's huge, I never say not to follow that desire wherever it goes. As a matter of fact, I would tell him or her to follow it anywhere because passion is the strongest thing in the world. You can't invent it, you can't ball it up and you can't make it in the lab. Passion is the most powerful resource you can ever have.

CHAPTER 2

MAKE YOUR GAME PLAN FOR SUCCESS

Once you've decided to change your mindset and begin the hard work of achieving your goals, the first thing you need to do is plant your flag. Make a game plan for success. Prioritize and prepare. And then be open-minded to receive the good things that are going to happen to you. You need to be ready to accept the responsibility of the success you achieve. Because you will achieve it.

Now you have your "why" and you are ready to start on the path to success. One of the first roadblocks people see is that they lack the power to achieve their goals. This is one of the biggest misconceptions I hear when I talk to people. They don't realize the incredible power that they already have.

Think about a housewife. We all know a housewife has one of the most important jobs anyone can do, but we don't think of a housewife as being as powerful as a general or a CEO. But consider everything a housewife does during a single day. First thing in the morning, she gets the house ready and makes breakfast for the kids. A kind word from mom can affect how the kids interact with their teachers and it can affect how they score on a test. Over time those kind words will determine how those kids see themselves. She sets the tone for the day and over time she sets the tone for her children's future.

Your kids really do emulate you no matter what. Children love their parents, and they do listen to what you say, although not always in the way you think. Talk with your kids, but also let them hear you talking with other people. When your children hear you talking to another parent whom they may hold in high regard as well about the dangers of drugs and alcohol, your kids will listen. This is a great way to communicate with your kids indirectly and often your message carries more weight than a lecture.

But back to our housewife. She's driving the kids to school in her SUV. She commands a 5,000 pound vehicle at 50 mph. And then maybe when she gets back home, she goes online to shop for groceries or clothes. Now she's determining the household spending and interacting with hundreds of people on the most powerful wealth-generating tool in history. Powerless? Not even close. Being a mom might be the most important job in America today because she builds the character of the next generation. More than anyone else, moms build our future as a society.

THE LESSON

Everybody has an opportunity to have a huge effect on somebody else. Some people might not think it, they may not understand the incredible power that they can have on somebody's life, but they absolutely have it.

You already have so much more power than you realize. One of the things I like to do when I speak is have someone bring in a big colorful wrapped box—like a Christmas present with a big bow—and place it in the front of the room. I tell the people, "You are such a great audience that I wanted to bring you all a gift. It's in this box and when we're done today I want to give it to you."

And you know how we all get when we know we're going to receive a present. I don't care how old you are. You get excited. "Oh, man. We're going to get something!" And because people like to receive gifts, they become a very attentive audience because now they're going to get a surprise at the end of my presentation.

What I tell them is that this gift has 99 percent of all the answers to their problems. And then they really start thinking, "Hmmm, the answers to all my problems. What in the world could this be?"

Then I open up that box and I bring out this gigantic mirror, the biggest one that will fit in the box. And I tell the audience to look into that giant mirror and they will see the answer to their problems. "The answer is right there, folks," I say. "Just look into this and you'll see it."

It's true. Everything you need to succeed in life, whether it's starting a business or advancing in your career or achieving a better balance between work and family, is inside you. But to achieve your goals, you need a game plan for success. Leadership is ultimately about helping others succeed, but before you can take care of No. 2 and No. 3, you need to take care of No. 1.

When my kids were young, one thing I would impress upon them is that if you don't accept responsibility, then you don't have freedom. When my kids were old enough to have a car, I helped them with a down payment, but they had a structured plan that they had to follow. They had to help pay for their auto insurance. They had to take care of the maintenance on the car (oil changes, inspections) and they had to have a monthly payment. That's how they found out what it's like to be an adult in this world. I didn't want to rob them of their freedom. They might have thought that freedom was, "Hey, I don't have a car payment." No. That's not what freedom is. Freedom is, "I have a car payment." How does that work? It works because I'm not depending on somebody else to do something. When you can do things for yourself, that's real freedom.

Don't be a parasite in this world. You become a free person by doing things for yourself, and that means paying your own bills. That's part of being free. I wanted my kids to learn this lesson, and today I'm so fortunate that my kids are wonderful young adults who just thrive on their independence. I'm so grateful for this because I know they're free now.

THE LESSON

Don't give up your freedom. When you lay your problems at the doorstep of somebody else, you've just given up your freedom.

I know what you're thinking. Success is for other people, those who got into the fancy schools, or knew somebody to get ahead or caught a lucky break. Well, think about General Colin Powell. He's one of the most impressive Americans I know. Powell was raised in the South Bronx and attended public school there. He graduated with a bachelor's degree in geology from City College of New York in 1958 with a C average and worked at a baby furniture story. Does this sound like the resume of a great general and statesman? After Powell finished his second tour in Vietnam in 1971, he got his MBA at George Washington University. We all think a four-star general has to have been an A student at West Point, but that is not always where it's at. Here's a guy who could have easily said, "Hey, the whole world's against me. I'm growing up as a black man in the South Bronx, the Civil Rights Movement is not even here yet, and this is tough."

Powell could have been the poster child for someone who had the deck stacked against him, someone born with two strikes, but he didn't act like that. Instead, he took responsibility for himself, became his own man and accomplished great things for our county.

THE LESSON

Someone who might seem by any measure to be a normal, average person can accomplish extraordinary things. If you accept the responsibility that comes with freedom, then you have the power to succeed, and all you have to do is find your passion center and then follow a game plan for achievement.

When you take on a task, you've got to break it out into steps. When your task is big—and all the best ones are—you've got to make a plan to accomplish it. When an architect is erecting a house or an office building, he doesn't just go out there with some nails and start hammering boards together. He's got to think about the structure. He's got to develop a blueprint for how he's going to build it. He's got to devote a lot of time and energy to develop this great task that he's going to do, so he's got to make it a big priority in his life. That's number one. You've got to prioritize. That's what I did in my baseball career after I talked with my dad about my throwing errors. I made fixing that the number one priority in my life. It was the most important thing in the world to me. It was actually more important than anything else that I could do, it was more important than anything my family could do. At that time, it was more important than anything in the world to me. That's a number one priority.

You set your priorities by listing the things that are important to you. Start with what's most important to you, and then ask yourself, "What's my 'why' again?" It always comes back to what's in your gut and what's in your heart.

STEVE'S TIP

Setting priorities before you begin working on a project is essential. If something is important to you, you have got to put it first in your life. For example, because of my family history, one of my top priorities is that I'm going to stay in shape. When I travel, it's important to me to be near a gym. And if there's no gym at the hotel and there's no opportunity for me to work out there, I'm going to stay at a different hotel. Staying in shape keeps my mind and my body working together. That's why I make sure to give myself an hour and a half every day to go and work out, and for that time I'm going to put everything else on the side because being healthy is so important to me.

Everything I've ever succeeded at was because I made the goal my number one priority. Remember, a goal is simply a dream with a deadline attached to it. Back when I was in high school in West Sacramento, I wanted a job at this restaurant so badly. It was a tiny Italian restaurant built in the 1930s called the Club Pheasant. It was one mile from my house and I was friendly with the family who owned the restaurant, so I knew that they would be flexible with my work schedule because playing baseball was another priority of mine. Professional baseball was still the No. 1 long-term goal. The problem with the restaurant job was that I was 14 years old and you had to be 16 to work there. Well, I just put it in my head when I was 14 years old that there's nothing else I'm going to think about other than that restaurant job. I'm not going to think about another job. I'm not going to think about a different place to work. It was just such a perfect job for me and I was going to get it no matter what anybody said.

I went in that restaurant week after week after week, and I kept asking them for a job. Finally one day they hired me. (Maybe they just got tired of me asking.) That job set the tone for me all through high school. I worked at this one job all through school. Three years and eight months. The family worked with me to accommodate my baseball schedule and it just couldn't have been a better situation. Everything that I thought out and planned, it all worked out perfectly. I made enough money at the restaurant so I could pay for my car, pay for my insurance, and pay for my own clothes.

The Club Pheasant is still there today. It's a thriving family-owned business. Definitely make a stop there the next time you're in West Sacramento. You won't be disappointed.

THE LESSON

Being a professional baseball player was my ultimate goal, but to accomplish your ultimate goal, you need to achieve a lot of smaller goals first. My family was pretty poor so I had to have a job to pay for things. So to get the restaurant job, I made it a priority, I prepared a plan to get the job, I stayed enthusiastic about the work, and I had an open mind to take advantage of the opportunity when it came. The method I applied when I was 14 years old to get that job was the exact same method I used to achieve success in baseball and business. One of the most amazing things I've ever read was what Helen Keller said when she was asked if being blind was the worst thing that could happen to a person. She replied, "The only thing worse than being blind is having sight but no vision." Situations might change. Principles don't. Those principles I applied when I was 14 years old are the same ones that guide me now in my career.

Even in this small example of a kid getting a job at an Italian restaurant, you can see how your mindset determines success—what you concentrate on and think about the most is going to grow the most. It doesn't matter what it is. Whatever you're concentrating on and thinking about the most will grow the most. That's what a priority is.

The next step is that you have to prepare for your task. What does that mean? The architect who's going to build that building, he's going to have to learn about the land on which he wants to build. He's going to have to talk with topography experts and find out exactly what is underneath the ground. He's going to have to find out if there's water under there. He's going to have to find out if there are any faults and if the ground is solid. He's going to have to do all of that preparation before he goes in and actually starts building.

The same is true with how you prepare to achieve your long-term goals. You cannot waiver one inch on preparation. It's the most critical element of achieving success because if you're building this thing on sand it's going to crumble. If your plan is built on rock then the foundation will be so stable that it will get you through those shaky times.

Think about courageous sea explorers like Ferdinand Magellan and Christopher Columbus. They didn't just get in their ships, raise the sails and go wherever the wind blew them. Seafaring was dangerous business in those days and those guys needed to be prepared. They talked with astrologers so they would know how to guide their ships by the stars, they met with cartographers to create navigation plans, and they had to make sure they brought enough food for their long journeys. Magellan and Columbus knew that the time you spend preparing is directly proportional to the size of the task ahead of you. The more ambitious your goal, the more you need to prepare.

Preparation is the part where you sacrifice, the part where you put in the most effort. The preparation is what people are going to notice. It is really the blood and guts of all your achievements.

The preparation phase is where you commit your time to your goals, where you sacrifice and where you learn the most. For my career in baseball, my true preparation took place when I was arriving early to the ballpark and staying late in the Arizona Fall League. Arizona is where major league clubs bring their top young players to elevate them faster through more intense and intricate baseball training after the regular minor league season is over.

Let me tell you, the system works. I learned more about baseball in a condensed period of time in the Arizona Instructional League than I did anywhere else in my whole career and those lessons made me a much better ballplayer.

The Dodgers brought me to Arizona in 1979 because I was just learning a new position. I'd never played second base in my life. I was always an outfielder and a shortstop, but the team believed that I'd be a candidate to play second base, so they sent me down to the Arizona Instructional League at the end of the summer.

I had no money. You hardly make any money in the Arizona league, so you have to just do the best that you can. I got paid enough money to live at a motel right on a highway, in one room with a little refrigerator in it. The rate was $50 per week, maybe even less. I don't remember exactly, but it wasn't a lot of money because I was sharing the room with the cockroaches.

Every morning I'd get up at about 6 a.m. I didn't have a car so I would walk to the ballpark, which was about a two-mile hike. I would get to the ballpark, and I would meet one of the coaches there. We had to be dressed for practice by 9 a.m., so I would get there at about 7 a.m. to meet with the coaches and they would teach me intricate details about hitting. In these early morning sessions, I was getting an edge on other players. Because I was dedicated to getting better, I was picking up things that other hitters didn't know and that helped me make it to the major leagues.

I would start hitting in the batting cages from 7:30 until about 9 a.m., and I would learn more about hitting than I ever dreamed possible. I would do this every day, and then afterward, I would change into another uniform because we had to start the regular practice at 9 a.m. We'd have a break at about noon and I would eat my lunch. The

Dodgers also had cereal in the morning for people who got there early, so I was getting two meals a day at the ballpark. When you're trying to live on a shoestring, two free meals at work are pretty cool.

So I'd eat cereal, and I'd eat whatever they served at lunch. Then we'd have the practice or a game that started at 1 p.m. That was over at about 4:30 p.m. Then I would stay after practice and take ground balls until it started getting dark. I would walk home, and there in my little motel room I made myself a bologna sandwich and a glass of orange juice for dinner. Every single night that's what I did.

The next day I would walk to the park and do the same thing all over again. One day I had an abscessed tooth and I had to go to the dentist. Somebody drove me to the dentist's office and dropped me off on one of the occasional off-days we had during the season. It was still really hot in Arizona because you got there in September after the minor league season ended in August.

I saw the dentist and he said, "OK, I can give you a root canal because you have an abscessed tooth, which costs $420, or I can pull out your tooth for $25." Well, I had no insurance and I didn't have any money, so he had to pull out my tooth.

After I got the tooth pulled, I had this big gauze in my mouth and I started walking back to my motel. It was really hot so I sat in the shade for a little bit, and the next thing I knew I woke up at 9 o'clock at night. It was dark and I walked home, about a two mile walk on the highway, on the side of the road, blood gushing from the big hole in my mouth.

No money, no wheels, no girlfriend. People think that professional athletes have it made and that they all make a gazillion dollars. They don't see the 99 percent of pro athletes who are in the minor leagues like that idiot walking along a highway holding bloody gauze against his mouth.

That's the kind of sacrifice you need to make when you prepare for success. I became a much better baseball player in Arizona because I had one-on-one attention, and I got the opportunity to put what I was learning into practice. Every day I was there at 7 a.m.—every single day without exception—for an hour and a half of hitting. Well, that's a lot of hitting. The blisters on my hands would bleed from all that hitting, but I was willing to do what other people were not willing to do. That's why I made it.

There were a lot of players in the minor leagues who were more talented that I was. They had more physical gifts, but I beat them because I had more desire. I out-hearted them.

I succeeded as a professional baseball player because of those long days I spent in the Arizona Instructional League. But remember, there are no guarantees that you're going to make it. They could have easily said, "Sax, you're out of here, you're gone." I had already lost the opportunity to go to college on a scholarship when I signed a professional contract. You have to be able to burn those bridges, put yourself on the line, and be willing to accept whatever happens. That's what preparing for success is all about.

When Napoleon Hill was writing *Think and Grow Rich*, he found that a very few people were actually living with a definite purpose in their lives. Economic hardship was robbing people of their hopes and dreams. Hill wrote, "What a different story people would tell if only they would adopt a definite purpose, and stand by that purpose until it became an all consuming obsession for success."

THE LESSON

Preparation is the critical point in your journey toward success. The preparation phase is when you put that burning desire in your heart to work. This is when you learn everything you need to know to achieve your dream and create a plan for everything you need to do. There are no guarantees you'll achieve your goal, but if you've prepared fully and put your heart and soul into it, you'll be in the very best position to succeed.

The other important thing about preparation is that it allows you to remove the shackles of pressure from yourself. If you're reading this book, you probably aren't the kind of person who goes too easy on yourself. But you might be the person who puts too much pressure on yourself to complete the project or get the sale. If you've fully prepared for the task at hand, then you've done everything you can to ensure success. Don't worry about things you can't control.

The first thing is to think of your long-term plan for success as a five-year plan. It's not going to happen tomorrow and it's not going to happen next week, so you've got to know that you have some time.

Keep your eye on your long-term goals. If you're beginning a new career, you have to create at least a five-year plan to really succeed. It takes about 10,000 hours of practice to be really successful at anything. At 40 hours a week, that means about five years.

When you're taking on a new job or you're starting your own business, you need to allow yourself a five-year plan to be successful. I saw that in baseball. Most guys spend at least five years in the minor leagues before they come up to the big leagues. The thing about pro sports that many people don't understand is that game day isn't difficult for the players. The game is the easy part. The game is fun. All the pressure, the time commitment, the sacrifice and the stress happen in practice. During the game, you're on automatic. You can't be thinking out there. You have to be on autopilot.

STEVE'S TIP

Whatever your long-term goal is, you must create a business plan to achieve it. Look at your goal like a factory. You have to go in and you have to put in so many hours, and you have to learn so much, and you have to make regular progress toward your goal. Always look at the finish line on the horizon, the end point where you want to get, and then work backward. "Where do I want to be in the fifth year? At the end of my fifth year, do I want to be right here?" And then just keep going back to the fourth year, the third year and so on. Once you have your plan, you'll want to check it quarterly, the way you do with your finances. You're like the mole who's digging in the ground, and you're just going and going and going and pretty soon you look up and you see where you are, and then you dig some more, and then you look up and see where you are. You know that you have a long way to go when you start out, and that's OK. You just do it incrementally.

Successful people are the ones who do the things most people won't do. I found that in finance, I found it in sports, I find it in public speaking. It's the stuff in the middle, between where you are now and where your goal is, the price you have to pay, the work, the studying, the time you put in, and the sacrifice. All those things in the middle are what I call minutia because they're really not a big deal. They're absolutely conquerable. So they're minutia. But people who don't do those things in the middle, people who have better things to do than study and prepare, those are the people who aren't going make it. That's just the way it is. The ultimate focus needs to be on the prize instead of the price.

STEVE'S TIP

Take the pressure off yourself and focus on what you can accomplish today. Think about how you can better yourself right now and tomorrow will take care of itself.

The other part of removing the shackles of pressure is to recognize that you can't control everything. Physically and mentally, you can only do as much as you can with what God gave you. That's it—you can't do anything more than that. I hear a lot of people in sports talk about giving 110 percent. Well, you can't do that. Because you're passionate and your "why" is big, you're going to give it 100 percent. There's no 110 percent because you can only give what you have and what you're capable of. You can train a donkey but I can guarantee you it's never going to win the Kentucky Derby.

If I give everything I possibly can—100 percent—then I don't worry about the numbers after that because it's not in my hands. That's in God's hands. I can only worry about what I can do. If it's not good enough, I am still completely happy with the result.

I can honestly say that I'm happy because it's not the outcome that matters. It's the effort. If you've given your best effort and fully committed yourself, that's all you can do. I told my kids the same thing when they were in school. I said, "I don't care what kind of grades you get. All I care about is how you prepare and how you go after it because in the end, you're only as good or great or as bad as what God gave you."

Just don't ever cheat yourself. That's one thing I can say in my career. I never cheated myself. If you never cheat yourself, then you just have to live with the results. If those results are not what you want, then you need to find another goal.

In a practical sense you just can't control the outcome of something beyond the effort you give. If you're giving 100 percent, you're prepared, you're doing it with enthusiasm, you made your goal your number one priority, and you did everything you're supposed to do, then you've done your part. Your mindset should be, "I can't really control everything in my life. I can control how I prepare for it. I can control my priority, and I can go at it with enthusiasm, so I've got that controlled. But ultimately, I can't really control the outcome. I can only control what I can do."

Some people drive themselves crazy because their mindset won't let them accept that they can't control everything. Trust me, you can't. So don't worry about that part you can't control and take that pressure off yourself because it's not helping you.

THE LESSON

Success is not going to happen overnight. You have to allow yourself at least five years or 10,000 hours to become successful at something new because there's always going to be a learning curve. People who sacrifice the most and try the hardest are going to get past that learning curve the fastest. Also, don't waste time worrying about things you can't control. If you've prioritized, you've prepared and you're working with enthusiasm, then you've done everything in your control to be in the best position for success. Accept that you can control those things in your power, but you can't control outcomes.

I tell people all the time to accept that there are things outside their control and remove the shackles of pressure from themselves. All you can control is what you have in front of you, and what you have to do. All you can control is the task is before you. That's it. You can't control all the other things that happen in the world. You can't control what people might think or what they might say. Focus your energy on those things you can control. I tried to do this in baseball and I've kept thinking about this throughout my career in business and public speaking.

I don't necessarily put a lot of importance on numbers. In a general sense, I have an idea of where I want to wind up as far as numbers go, but quite often when we do that, we're lowering the bar for ourselves or we're holding ourselves back. We're minimizing what we could do. You've heard the saying, "Don't make your minimum your maximum." I really believe that.

If you go out and just do the best you can do, and you can look in the mirror and say, "I gave 100 percent effort to this task," then the numbers are going to be what they are. And lots of times they're going to be better than you thought they'd be. So let that pressure go and accept that you can't control everything. You'll find that it becomes easier to control the things you can.

Once you've prioritized and prepared, you don't just have a dream anymore, you have a purpose. You've made this purpose a priority in your life and you've done the preparation so now you know what it's going to take to achieve this purpose. Now you need to stand by that purpose until it becomes an all-consuming obsession for success. That's right, I said, "Obsession." For a lot of people that word has a negative connotation, but it's a lot like peer pressure. There's a good kind of peer pressure and a bad kind of peer pressure. The same is true of obsessions.

Think about all the people in the world. Everyone you've ever known or read about. Now think about the really, really, *really* successful people. They are a little bit different than other people. I believe that the people who are really, really successful in their lives are obsessed with achieving success. And if you want to be successful in any endeavor in your life, you have to be obsessed with it.

When some people hear the word "obsession," they instinctively recoil from it because it sounds extreme and in today's politically correct world anything extreme is a horrible thing. Believe me, there's nothing wrong with obsession. If you're a successful person, there are going to be times in your life where you're obsessed with something, but ironically it's because of that obsession that later on you will achieve the balance that we all are looking for in our lives. We want to have time with our families. We want to have time for work. We want to have time for vacation. We want to have personal time. And sometimes we have to be obsessed with something to create a life in which we have time for all those other important things.

STEVE'S TIP

Make sure you are getting the right advice from the right people. I believe personal-development books are outstanding sources of advice. Try to read something from a personal-development book every day—even if only for a half-hour. These books will help you stay focused on your goals and create positive actions every day.

I talk a lot about how success happens over time—which it does—but you still need to have a sense of urgency about your goals. Try this game with me. Let's say you have your goal in your mind, and now I want you to imagine it's the Old West and you need to choose your mode of transportation to get to your goal. There are three different ways that you can travel.

The first way is to ride Eeyore, the donkey from *Winnie the Pooh*. Well, you know that won't work. You're not going to get anywhere very fast riding Eeyore, and I don't know if you're going to get very far. I'm not so sure I would want to ride Eeyore anyway because he was a complainer – a very negative little donkey.

The second way is to ride a field pony. You can ride a field pony and you could probably get to your destination on one. But it might take you an awful long time to get there, because field ponies aren't very fast, they just kind of just tread along.

The third way you could go is to ride on the Pony Express. From 1860-1861, the Pony Express was the fastest mail service ever seen in the West, delivering mail from St. Joseph, Mo., to Sacramento, Ca., in ten days with an almost flawless record despite regularly traveling through dangerous Indian territory. Only one piece of mail was ever lost on the Pony Express, and the only thing that could beat its speed was the transcontinental telegram. That's how you want to be traveling toward your goals: on the Pony Express. Fearless, fast and dependable.

STEVE'S TIP

When I'm hiring people, I look for leaders. I'm trying to find leaders with whom I want to work. I want to find leaders who are willing to do what it takes to be successful, who have their own priorities as far as what they want to do and how fast they want to get there. If somebody looks ready for the Pony Express, that's the person I want to ride with. Remember that a company's best resource is not its technology, its marketing or its flagship product. A company's most important resource is its personnel, the human element of the whole enterprise. It's the spirit and ingenuity of their workforce!

That's why I'm such a huge fan of Donald Trump. You can point out many successful people in the world today, but Trump is the standard bearer. He easily could have stayed in Brooklyn and sold brownstones with his father Fred, but he wanted to conquer Manhattan. In his No. 1 national bestseller *Trump: The Art Of The Deal*, Trump writes about the importance of creating ambitious goals for yourself: "I like thinking big. I always have. To me it's very simple: if you're going to be thinking anyway, you might as well think big. Most people think small because most people are afraid of success, afraid of making decisions, afraid of winning. And that gives people like me a great advantage."

As a member of the New York Yankees, I've met Trump several times at Yankee Stadium and I have heard him give a keynote speech many more times. But when you peel back all of his impressive accomplishments, the thing I admire most about Trump is that he likes to have fun. In *Trump: The Art Of The Deal*, he writes, "I don't kid myself. Life is very fragile, and success doesn't change that. If anything, success makes it more fragile. Anything can change, without warning, and that is why I try not to take any of what's happened too seriously. Money was never a big motivation for me, except as a way to keep score. The real excitement is playing the game." Trump personified!

You want to create high expectations for yourself. Successful people consistently raise the bar of what's expected of them, they raise what they ask of themselves. That's an important outlook to have if you want to grow in your business and as a person. Challenge yourself. Look at someone like the swimmer Michael Phelps. You talk about a guy who is always raising the bar. He breaks the world record and then he's out there training hard because he wants to break it again. He wants to break his own record! That's how you challenge yourself. Find out the best you can possibly do at something, and the next time, try to do it even better.

You must demand and expect the best from yourself. I don't understand why people try to negotiate the price of success. I don't get that. Why do we accept mediocrity, from ourselves or others? Whatever it takes to be successful, that's the price you have to pay, not a dime or an hour of practice less.

You always hear that practice makes perfect, but that's not entirely true. Practice doesn't make perfect, but *perfect practice* makes perfect.

Practice is one of the most overlooked tools that we can use in any endeavor. You know which skills you need to succeed in your field, so why not practice them so you can be at your very best. It seems so simple, but many of us neglect practice, especially as we get older. That's a mistake. No matter how successful and accomplished you are in your field, you can always improve. There's always something you can get better at. So get out there and practice.

The key to practicing something is to not just go through the motions. You need to have perfect practice to really improve. If you're out there and you're doing your thing, and you're practicing, but not really doing it correctly, you're going to do more harm than good. You're going to ingrain your bad habits. You're going to be practicing and instilling the wrong way of doing things.

Everybody who is a professional—no matter what they're doing— they know what is right and what is wrong. They know that if they have a test, for example, and it's an open-book test, that there are two ways that you can take that open-book test. You could just go right to the test and take it, or you can actually print out the material, study it, and spend the three or four hours getting to know the subject matter, become confident that you understand it, and then take the test. We all know that there's a right way and a wrong way to do everything. It's just a matter of committing yourself to doing things the right way every day. That's the mindset for success.

When I was playing baseball, I got over my throwing problem because I knew the correct way to field and throw a ball so I was able to practice it every day. If I was not doing that practice correctly, if I was what they call olé-ing the ball, where you field it off to the side with one hand like a matador instead of fielding the ball in the center of your body with two hands, I wouldn't have gotten better. You know the right and wrong way to do things. So you have to make sure that you're practicing correctly. It's so important. When you practice correctly, it instills good habits and it breeds confidence because you know if you're doing it right in practice, you'll carry it on through the game, the meeting, or the sales call.

STEVE'S TIP

When I have a major speech or sales meeting that I must prepare for, I always tell myself the following: "You might talk better, sell better or look better than me, but you CANNOT outwork me, you CANNOT silence my spirit, you CANNOT control my will and you CANNOT stop me from learning." You can make money or you can make excuses but you CANNOT make both.

Practice isn't just for activities like baseball. Let's talk about parenting. Say you're supposed to take your kid to school and you wake up late, you don't even make their lunch, you drop them off at school, and your son missed 20 minutes of his first period and he gets a tardy notice. Pretty soon the teacher will be calling you up and saying, "Hey, your kid's been tardy all the time. What's the problem?" Well, the problem is that you're not practicing your parenting skills very well.

As a parent, as a leader and as a team member, you need to be an example, and you have to practice correctly. If you don't practice correctly, it's going to have a ripple effect. You're not going to be as good as you want to be, and it will affect the people around you in a negative way. So you need to practice, and you need to practice correctly.

THE LESSON

Perfect practice means putting in the extra time to make sure you are working to the best of your abilities. Success and struggle go together like calories and donuts. Anytime somebody has done something really successful, they worked hard. There are a lot of people who are interested in a lot of things, but the people who find success are the ones who are *committed*, not just "interested." If you make a commitment and you're willing to pay the price, you'll find the rewards will make the struggle worth it.

CHAPTER 3

CREATING THE SUCCESSFUL ATTITUDE

Let's go to a football game together. The stadium is full and the cheerleaders are waving their pom-poms and the players are on the field. You and I are up in the stands with some hot dogs. Now look down and tell me what you see, OK?

We have the interior linemen. They're all about 6'5", 6'6". They weigh about 300 pounds. They all look alike. What about the wide receivers? Let's see. Well, they're all tall. They're about 6'2" to 6'5". They run like the wind, and they can jump like crazy, and they've got great hands to catch the football. What about the running backs? Well, they're about 6'1" or 6'2". They weigh around 230 pounds, and they've got great starting ability to go left and right, and file forward. The quarterbacks are tall, lanky guys who can see down the field and throw the ball far. Linebackers might be the best athletes out there because they're a mixture of everything. They're fast. They're agile. They're big.

So what's the difference? When we're sitting up here looking down at the game, all these guys are the same. They all look the same. They all run the same. They do everything the same. So what makes the difference between a Walter Payton or a Peyton Manning and an unknown also-ran? What makes one guy an all-star, and another guy just another guy? It's what they have in their ribcage. Your heart and your passion make the difference, bud. They make all the difference in the world.

THE LESSON

I don't care if it is a football field, a baseball diamond or a basketball court. I don't care if it's an office building. I don't care if it's the best truck driver in town or the best barbecue man in town. Whatever it is, heart and passion are going to separate someone who's successful and an all-star in their field from someone who's just another guy or just another woman. There is no question in my mind about that. That's what the edge is. That's what makes the difference.

Here's another example of how much heart matters. You know the difference between a guy that hits .260 in the big leagues and the guy who's going to the Hall of Fame and hitting .300?

It's one big hit a week. Think about this. There are 26 weeks in a baseball season. Let's say your batting average is based on about 500 at-bats. That's 26 hits. That's one hit a week that makes the difference between a guy who is going to the Hall of Fame and a guy who was an also-ran.

If you start at the beginning of the baseball season, opening day, and you take the best team in baseball, the team that's going to win the World Series and you take the worst team, the one that's going to finish in the cellar, I can tell you one thing right now: each of those teams is going to win 54 games, and each of those teams is going to lose 54 games. The World Series champion and the cellar-dweller. They're both going to win 54 and lose 54.

So what's the difference? It's those other 54 games. And it's going to come down to little, tiny things that will make the difference between wins and losses. The smallest things can make the difference in a baseball game. And when you play with heart you do those tiny, little things. You give me somebody who has talent, and you give me a guy who has less talent but more heart, the guy with more heart is going to win every single time. Look at it this way: not everybody can run for two 40-yard touchdowns in a game. Even the guy who did it can't do it the next game. We all have ups and downs, but nobody ever had a slump in hustling.

That's why the guy with heart always wins in the end, because you don't have slumps in hustling. That supersedes any boundaries. Hustle shows just how much you want something. If you always go at things with intensity and hustle, then you're going to be able to ride through some tough times.

There are times where we all make mistakes in whatever we're doing, but if we work with a lot of hustle and a lot of intensity, we can override some of our shortcomings just by going out and getting it done with passion and intensity.

Edwin Barnes was like that when he went to see Thomas Edison. There was nothing remarkable about Barnes except for what was in his heart. Take a guy like Pete Rose. If you put Pete Rose in a tryout camp today, he might not even get drafted because he couldn't run; he had average power, no throwing arm, and average fielding skills. He could hit, but he wasn't blessed with great speed. Seriously, today's scouts might have passed on Rose, but he's someone who might be one of the 10 greatest players who ever played, all because of what was in his heart

If you ever saw Pete Rose play baseball, there was no mistaking how much passion and heart he had for the game. Here's something to think about: your heart and passion show in how you do your job just as clearly as it did when Pete Rose played baseball. If I watch a person work day in and day out at their job, I can pretty much tell you what kind of person they are on the inside by watching them work. I can see the way that they approach their job or approach their business. I can see their interaction with other people. I can see the self-respect that they carry in themselves by the way that they approach their vocation. I can see the way they handle stress. I can see the way that they attack their job and their passion. I can see what they do in between spurts of working, like how they handle their downtime at work. I can just see all these different elements that create a fabric of what kind of a person they are. So I can watch a person work for a day and get a good idea of what kind of person they are. I'm sure you can too. It's the same thing as being able to tell that Pete Rose hustled on the ball field.

When I watch successful people work, I see that they all have confidence, they all create structure in their lives, and they all have integrity. Those are the things I watch for because if someone possesses those traits I know he or she is destined to succeed.

THE LESSON

Success isn't just about how you perform at the big meeting or the sales call. You achieve success through the little things you do every day. It's the tedious little things you must do with passion every day that are going to make the difference, the same way Pete Rose got his 4,256 hits, one at a time.

Once you have your goal, and you know your why, you'll find that your heart will be engaged in everything you do. Now you need to apply that passion to the task at hand. That means being 100 percent committed to achieving your goal and to those daily tasks that through your preparation you know you need to complete to get there.

Sometimes when I'm doing one of my speeches, I'll set up a small table in front of the audience and I'll put a light on this table. And I'll invite some lady from the audience up. I hold her hand, I pull out the chair for her, and I sit her at the table. It looks like we're on a little date and everybody's watching.

I tell her that we've got to pretend we're a couple and we're out on a date. She says OK. So we're role-playing. So I start by saying, "It's just so great to be with you and I'm just so in love with you, and we're thinking about our future, and do you want to live at the beach, or do you want to live in the city? And what should we name our children? Oh my God, we've got all these wonderful things to think about." The crowd starts laughing and getting into it because everybody responds to a love story.

Then I drop this on her. I say, "You know what? Honey, I'm just so excited about our life together. I'm telling you right now that I can commit to you 99 percent of the time. What do you think?" You hear some rumbling from the crowd, and the woman—no matter how many times I've done this—always says, "No, I'm not doing that."

Now the woman goes back to her chair and everybody gives her a nice round of applause. Then I say, "Folks, would anybody buy this bag of worms? Would anybody go along with this shyster who's only going to be committed to this lady 99 percent of the time?" Everybody says, "No way!" Then I ask, "So why do you make that same deal with yourself in your other endeavors in your life?"

THE LESSON

You're either committed or you're not. There's not a gray area. It's a yes-or-no answer to a very simple question. Yet there are so many people in this world who are 99 percent committed or maybe less than that. Nobody is going to buy that. You wouldn't accept that from someone else, so why would you make that same deal with yourself?

If you're in a position right now in your job and you do not like it and you're not getting it done at work, and you're just hanging in there, working just long enough so that you don't get fired, then why are you making that same deal with yourself?

If you want to do something different in your life, you need to get up and change it. You need to change the way you're doing things. You need to change the way you're thinking. You need to change the way you're going about your business. You need to change your mindset in life. You have got to change it because 99 percent is not going to cut it.

Success is all about being committed to your goals and the task at hand. Now, some people are bothered when they see someone who has an intense commitment to his or her goal. When you've committed to your goal 100 percent, people are going to question you. Sometimes people see someone committed to a goal and say, "Whoa! You're hyper." The one that really gets me is when somebody tells me, "Why don't you just relax?" That drives me up a wall. I know how to relax. And it's always the most negative people who say this. Sometimes I talk about this in my speeches. I ask people if they are excited and happy, and when I see those negative people and they tell me, with a long face and a less-than-enthusiastic mumble, "Yes, I'm happy." I say, "Well, you better tell your face, because I'm not seeing it."

The best way to distinguish between interest and commitment, between someone who would like to succeed but isn't willing to put in the necessary work and someone who will do whatever it takes to accomplish his or her dreams is to think about having a backbone instead of a wishbone. You need to have a backbone, not a wishbone to succeed. Success takes strength and a wishbone just isn't going to cut it.

So once you've committed your heart 100 percent to your goal, the final part of creating an attitude for success is patience. Remember that achieving success is a small series of steps; it's not a giant leap. If there's one thing you need to remember, it's that there is no such thing as overnight success. In fact, people who demonstrate patience are more likely to succeed than those people who want it all five minutes ago. Those people looking for the quick fix have wishbones and you know that you need a backbone to succeed in life.

STEVE'S TIP

Keep your eye on the horizon. You have to be focused on the end point. Getting too involved in your day-to-day problems and hiccups is not going to be advantageous. There are going be times when you don't want to do this, but if your mind is focused on your long-term goal, you'll be able to keep those daily ups and downs in perspective.

The link between patience – that is, the ability to delay instant gratification in order to achieve more in the long-term – and success was proved in a decades-long Stanford University study. In his renowned book *Don't Eat the Marshmallow…Yet!* author Joachim De Posada outlined this 30-year year study of human behavior. The psychologists at Stanford wanted to discover the mental processes that make some people delay instant gratification. In other words, they wanted to identify self-control.

In the test, the scientist took a kid into a room—the kids were about 4 to 6 years old—and said, "Sit right here and, by the way, here's a marshmallow that I'm going to put in front of you."

Then the kid hears the rules. The scientist says, "Listen, I will be back in 15 minutes. You can eat this marshmallow if you want, but if you wait fifteen minutes until I come back, I'm going to give you another marshmallow so you'll have two marshmallows."

Then the scientist leaves the room and watches what the kids do on video. I've seen these videos and they are heartbreaking and funny at the same time. Some of the kids took the marshmallow and smelled it and licked it. One of the kids was brilliant; he made a little hole in the marshmallow and sucked out the middle of it, and then propped it back up on the table to look like the whole marshmallow was still there. Can you imagine when you're 5 years old trying not to eat a marshmallow that was right in front of you?

What the study found over 30 years was fascinating. By a huge margin, the kids who resisted eating the marshmallow were far more successful later in life than the kids who ate the marshmallow. If they had the self-control at 5 years old to hold off eating one marshmallow so they could get two, they could also delay gratification so they could study hard to do well in school and work hard to advance in their career.

This study tells us a couple things. Most importantly, it shows us that what you do early in your kid's life is so important. This study tested kids between the ages of 4 and 6 and already the roots of their future life were firmly planted.

What else do we learn from this study? People who are patient achieve lasting success. Sure, all these kids had to do was wait 15 minutes, but to a kid a 15-minute wait is like three or four adult hours. I just love that study, because it shows how much of human behavior is so obvious. You can slice and dice it and come up with all these great scientific words and descriptions, but human behavior is not that hard to figure out. If you want to be successful, you have to learn self-control and how to delay gratification.

For a kid it's a marshmallow, but for you it could be the many distractions that get in the way of achieving your goal. If there's one thing our 21st century world is good at creating, it's distractions that keep our minds off our goals.

THE LESSON

You need heart and passion to succeed, but you also need discipline and self-control in applying that passion. When you can do that, you'll find you'll have all the marshmallows you could ever want.

CHAPTER 4

GET OVER YOURSELF

HUMILITY, RESPONSIBILITY AND INTEGRITY WILL CARRY THE DAY

n August of 1981, when I was 21, I got called up to the big leagues as a Los Angeles Dodger. I played around 20 games, enough to know that I could play at this level. The Dodgers were getting ready to go to the World Series that year and our manager Tommy Lasorda brought me into his office and said, "Look, I've got to play the veteran guy." When I got called up, the Dodgers' regular second baseman Davey Lopes had been hurt. Now Davey was healthy and Tommy said he needed to play Davey to get him ready for the post-season because we were already going to the playoffs.

"But I will tell you that if I'm the manager next year, you're going to be the second baseman," Tommy said. "I give you my word."

That's just about the best thing a young ballplayer could hear, so for the rest of the season I was just going to shut up and do my thing. So it's now a couple games before the end of the season, and Tommy was starting to play Davey to get him ready for the playoffs. But then Davey got himself kicked out of the game for something, so I had to go in the game and replace him. This was in the Houston Astrodome late in September 1981, and the Astros pitcher, Don Sutton, was going for his 56th career shutout. It would have been a record. He already had 55, and he was beating us 4-0.

I had just got called into the game, and I was the last guy up, and I had two strikes on me. I remember a couple things so clearly from that night. Number one, the Astrodome was sold out, and 60,000 people were chanting along with that big Astrodome score-board flashing, "Strike him out! Strike him out! Strike him out!" And

I was down in the count: one ball, and two strikes. Suddenly Don Sutton threw me a fastball and all I did was just react. I just turned and threw the head of the bat and, man, I hit a line-drive bullet out of the park for a homerun.

I couldn't act like I was overjoyed because we were losing the game. I wanted to jump up out of the Astrodome I was so happy, but I just rounded the bases, all business, and went back into the dugout. Then Sutton got the next batter out, and that was the end of the game.

So I'm in the dugout taking my gloves off and getting ready to walk up through the underpass of the stadium to the clubhouse with the rest of my teammates. Before I could even get out of the dugout, somebody tapped me on the shoulder and I looked over. Don Sutton was sitting right next to me. And he had the baseball that I just hit a homerun off of him with. He came up to me and he said, "I'm going to tell you something. I've seen a lot of young players come up and I want to tell you that I think you're going to have a huge career, and I want to congratulate you for hitting this homerun off me. And I'm going to sign this baseball and give it to you."

And Don Sutton did that for me. It was amazing. I had just hit a homerun off the guy and yet there he was finding the ball and signing it for me. It was as graceful an act of sportsmanship and professionalism on the part of Don Sutton as I'd ever witnessed before or since, and for a young rookie just learning my way in baseball, Sutton showed me how to act in the game.

THE LESSON

Don Sutton showed me how to play baseball with class. There's a professional way to do things in every field, and doing things the professional, old-fashioned way is the coolest thing you can do. Don showed me how a leader shows respect and admiration for others, and to this day I take his example to everything I do in my life.

Now let's compare the class of a player like Don Sutton with the narcissism we see in baseball today. The big slugger comes up to bat in his extra-baggy uniform and the 17 pounds of body armor that he's wearing so he doesn't get hit by the pitch. The reason he wears that baggy uniform, by the way, is that it would be impossible for a snug-fitting uniform to hold that much muscularity. It just would be beyond comprehension. That's why he must wear the baggy uniform. And believe me, if he could sag the pants, he would. You can see him step into the box and slightly dig in. The slugger hits the homerun, and freezes in his glorious follow-through. First of all, he wants everybody to see the statuesque manner in which he stands there and watches the ball go out of the ballpark. He cannot put his arms down from his follow-through because he is just as enamored of the flight of the ball as everybody else in the stands. So he just stands there with this statue-like pose in his follow-through as he watches the ball fly out of the ballpark, and kisses himself up and down those powerful arms. Then you see him snap back to reality and realize that he must perform the daunting task of running around the bases.

So the slugger slow-trots to first. Before he gets to first base though, he has to let the first-base coach congratulate him with a stupendous high-five. So they do the high-five. Then the slugger slows himself back to a trot, the better which to let everybody glorify him. He hits first base, and then goes to second base. By this time he has pointed up to the Lord three or four times to make sure the Lord's watching as well. And then when he comes to third base, he low-fives the third-base coach because he wants to mix things up a little bit. Then he comes home, and points to the sky a couple more times. Got to make sure the Lord's still watching. And then he turns around to doff his cap to the fans and disappears into the dugout to a rousing standing ovation. That should do it, right? Nope. He waits to hear that chant—"One more time! One more time!"—and he comes back out. Takes off the cap again. Blows more kisses. Pirouettes back into the dugout, only to be seen again when he has to come out and take his position on defense. This whole thing takes seven or eight minutes. It should take 20 seconds.

All I can think when I watch this is, "Man, imagine if someone tried that on Nolan Ryan." My gosh, one time I tried to bunt on Nolan Ryan. Holy cow! You didn't try to bunt on Nolan Ryan. And if you hit a homerun off him, boy, watch out. Today, if you throw inside, they want to toss you out of the game. The umpire will warn both benches. "You, and you, you're warned!" No throwing inside? Are you kidding me? That's part of the game! If you took away throwing inside from Bob Gibson, if you took away throwing inside from Don Drysdale, these guys would have been .500 pitchers! They lived on intimidation. That's how you separate the weak from the strong in baseball. If you can intimidate those people, if you can get in their head, they're going to have a real hard time hitting the ball hard. Now today you can't do that. The umpires won't let guys pitch that way, the way you're supposed to pitch. That's why players today hit 50 homeruns, and that's why their batting averages are as high as they are. You can't intimidate anybody anymore. It's not politically correct. You might hurt the nurturing aspect of their psyche if you intimidate them.

STEVE'S TIP

You know we're in trouble when even baseball is getting politically correct. "Oh no, the pitcher might intimidate somebody. Does that mean they will need counseling?" As a society, we're getting away from our traditional bedrock values. It's important for you to adhere to these time-tested values because they will make you stand apart and people will respect you more. I'm not saying that all change is bad, because sometimes change is really good. However, when it comes to professionalism and leadership, those values are fixed and permanent. They don't vary according to fashion or the times.

Don't even get me started on soccer. I watched the World Cup and you see the same posturing and self-aggrandizement you do in baseball, but they add an international flair to the proceedings. Let's say someone is trying to kick the ball and they accidentally nick one of the opposing players. You can see it clearly on TV, he barely touches the guy, but, man, that guy goes down in a heap, holding his leg and screaming bloody murder. I mean, where's the ambulance? Then 15 seconds go by, he doesn't get the call and that same guy—the one screaming like someone who broke his leg in three places—just pops up and he's fine. He starts running around again. Are you kidding me?

If there's ever a fight in one of these sports, I want those soccer guys. That's the guy I want to be matched up against in the fight. After the game is over, it looks like a sniper took half these teams out, all these guys just laid out everywhere on their backs. I saw one guy just sitting on his knees, slumped back with his head in his hands, openly sobbing. I mean, he was sobbing, crying like a child. Then a guy from the other team comes up, brushes back the locks from his face, looks up, holds the other player's face in his hands—this is a grown man doing this!—and kisses his tear-soaked face, trying to give him some solace. Some comfort so he can get through the night because he just lost a soccer game.

Hey, there was a 50 percent probability when you stepped on the field that you were going to lose. We all know that somebody's going to win, and somebody's going to lose. You play your hardest, you give it your all, and when it's over, you accept the result. You don't cry. You don't fall on the field like you've been shot. Sometimes I can't believe what we're seeing in sports today. It can hurt to lose, but you don't make a spectacle out of yourself. If you've got feelings you need to get out, that's what the locker room is for.

STEVE'S TIP

Humility is not taking yourself too seriously, but taking what you do very seriously.

These examples show why sports have deteriorated as much as they have. And unfortunately this is not only a problem in professional sports. This is a human behavioral trait that just happens to be conspicuous in sports. But it's everywhere. I'm sure you see the same kind of behavior in your field of work. The liberal permissive attitude that we see in the world today is making our society come apart at the seams, and I think it's a huge contributor to our current problems, not only in the United States, but everywhere around the world.

The irony is that we're marginalizing ourselves through this self-glorification. When we're constantly blowing our own horns, we fail to show respect and admiration for others and their accomplishments. What we see in sports is a microcosm of where we are in society today. We have got to make sure that we don't lower the bar and jeopardize all those great things that we've created over our history as a nation.

The number one thing lost is *class*. When you lose your humility and your respect for the game and your opponents, you destroy the value of the game, which was the very reason we played it in the first place. Yes, take what you do seriously, but don't take yourself too seriously. That to me is the essence of humility. There's a greater purpose to why we're here in the world, and it's to help other people. When you make something all about you, then there really isn't much value to it.

STEVE'S TIP

There's a link between the way you carry your-selves and the way you do things. If you see someone slouched down, and wearing an untucked shirt and maybe baggy jeans and just looking dumpy, that's not someone who inspires a lot of confidence. If you are a leader and committed to your goals, it's important to dress the part.

Remember chivalry? That code of honor and manners that true gentlemen and ladies once held themselves to? I sometimes worry that too many people have forgotten what chivalry means and their obligation to act with chivalry in their lives. Fortunately, we get reminders from time to time that chivalry is not completely gone. One time about 10 years ago when I was still working in financial services, I was in Las Vegas for a business meeting and my son was with me. He was 13 years old at the time. A lady came into the meeting a few minutes late, and my son got up, walked to an empty seat at the table and pulled her chair out for her. I didn't ask him to, but he knew the right thing to do in that situation. The best way to keep chivalry alive is to act in that manner yourself. People will notice, and they will respect you for it.

I'm not just a nostalgic old-timer claiming that things were better in my day. I know a lot of great athletes today who still play the game with a lot of class. As a matter of fact, most athletes today don't display this kind of boorish behavior we've been talking about. But enough of them do and these selfish attitudes permeate throughout our society. I see Little League games. I see pickup basketball games and intramurals, and I see how these young kids respond to what they see on TV. Our children are looking to us to learn how to behave, which is why it's so important to take responsibility for our actions.

In 1994, I wrote a column for *The Wall Street Journal* about how permissive attitudes in society were negatively affecting our kids. What really got me to write that column is when I went to a school to talk to some eighth and ninth graders. I was just shocked to hear some of these kids' language and what they would say to a teacher. I would really say that part of it was the teacher's fault, because the teacher permitted this attitude in the classroom. That's where you have to draw boundaries and you have to put up fences for kids. Trust me, those kids want someone to make that distinction in their life because when kids grow up with no responsibilities and with no guidelines, they don't have any confidence. When kids grow up with guidelines and responsibilities and fences in their lives, then they grow up with a lot of confidence because they know that someone cares about them. That makes a big difference in life and kids who don't have the discipline in their lives know they are getting the short end of the stick.

So this visit to the school was what persuaded me to write the piece. Hearing the language and seeing the disrespect in that classroom helped me realize what we were losing through our lower standards, our shirking the responsibility of disciplining our children, and our refusal to teach our children right from wrong. I stopped one kid in his tracks. I said, "Listen, what you're doing here is terribly wrong." I told him that he didn't respect himself, and he certainly didn't respect his class or his teacher. And I told him that he was wrong. The kid looked shocked. I don't think he had ever been told he was "wrong" in his life.

The message of my column really resonated with people. In fact, I received a letter praising the column from the White House. The reason the column had this effect is because we all realize that as a society we're losing our moral compass. A lot of times what people do is they try to blame the school, or they try to blame the economy, or they try to blame this or that. But it really starts at home. It starts with us and how we accept our responsibilities as parents. The last thing I expected was to get a letter from the White House, which said that the President and the First Lady had read my column and that they really liked what I had said. But I just felt compelled to write it because I had such strong feelings after I went to that school. I was stunned by the disrespectful attitude and actions of the students there and how they could freely cuss in front of their schoolteacher.

There is a huge breakdown here. There's been a terrible change of attitude that I saw from the time I was a student in the classroom until now. And I don't like one bit where it was going. You need to respect people who are your teachers. You respect people who are trying to help you and your parents and your elders. When I saw the lowering standards in our schools, I was compelled to write that column, and I'm glad *The Wall Street Journal* printed it.

All of you with kids know that to be a good parent you need to have a lot of patience. It's real easy to say yes to your kid. It's easy just to give in. But I truly believe that you have to be a parent to your kids first and foremost, especially when they're young. You'll have time to be their friend later.

I'll give you an instance. My daughter was wearing clothes to school that didn't conform to her school's dress code. Nothing really bad at all. Maybe she had a shirt that had a spaghetti strap on it over the shoulder that the school didn't allow. Her school had a pretty strict dress code and she was expected to follow it. So I kept telling her, "Hey, we can go over to Ralph Lauren, we can go to Macy's, or Nordstrom, wherever you want. We'll get you some more clothes that are cool, but that would conform to your dress code at school." She wouldn't have any of it. So for about two or three weeks I kept after her. Then one morning I just walked into her room when she was just waking up. All she heard was this *whoosh!* sound. That was the sound of me taking her clothes off the hanger in her closet in one fell swoop, going right downstairs, outside to the garbage can and throwing those clothes in.

You know how important clothes are to a young girl. They mean *everything*. And boy, there was fire coming out of her ears. I said, "You know what? Right now you don't like me very much, but I have to be your parent. I have to be your parent and can't be your friend right now, but when you're a grownup, you and I are going to be really tight."

I was exactly right. My daughter and I are really, really close, and one of the main reasons is because when she was growing up I put up fences. There were guidelines, and she knew deep down how much I loved her because I wasn't willing to sacrifice what I knew was right for her. Even though it was hurting me to do it, I couldn't bend because it wasn't right for her. That's why patience is so important for parents.

THE LESSON

When you're a parent, there are times when you cannot be a friend. There are going to be times when it's going to be hard and you're going to have to be "the mean parent." And if you're in a two-parent family, then you're going to be leveraged against the other parent because "the other parent doesn't make me do this, but you do." But you know what's right, and you have to stand behind it. You have to do what you think is right. You have to be steadfast in those beliefs and know that to say, "Yes, OK" is the easy way out. You know in your heart what's right, and you have to stick by your convictions. That's true for anything that you're doing: at work, in your personal life, everything else. You have to stick by your personal core beliefs.

In addition to patience, you also need a sense of personal responsibility. What accepting responsibility means is not saying you're a victim of your circumstances, but rather using those circumstances to help you become the person you want to be. I sometimes think about a story I heard about these twin brothers. Their dad was a murderer, and he wound up in prison. One of the boys ended up just like his dad and he was asked, "Why did you follow your father into a life of crime and violence?" And he said, "My dad beat my mother. He beat my brother and me, and he never showed me any affection and he was horrible, so that's why I turned out like this."

But his twin brother didn't follow the same path. Instead the brother became a successful businessman, he married a lovely woman and they raised a family together. And he was asked, "Your father led a life of crime and violence, why did you lead such a good life?" And he said, "My dad beat my mother. He beat my brother and me, and he never showed me any affection and he was horrible, so that's why I turned out like this."

So this guy obviously took the same things that happened to his brother, which turned his brother into the same kind of person as his father, and he turned it into something positive. He was able to look at that and say, "Hey, that's not going to be me. I'm not going to be like that."

That's something I've done in my family, too. My dad was not an affectionate father. He just wasn't a touchy-feely type of a person. That's not what he was about. So I was just the opposite with my kids. I loved and respected my dad more than I could ever tell you, but I wanted to be affectionate with my children. I still hug and kiss my 22-year-old son in front of his friends. I don't mind. And my son doesn't mind, either.

THE LESSON

We're given a choice in life. We can take our experiences from our life, and we can use them whatever way that we want to. You can certainly choose to be a victim like the first brother. Or you could do what the other brother did and say, "You know what? That's the example I had, and it's exactly why I'm not going to be that way. I'm going to take my experiences and I'm going to turn them for the better." You have the ability to take your experiences and do what you want with them. It's your choice.

This idea of taking responsibility for your actions and showing backbone and resolve in the face of obstacles is the theme of one of my favorite poems.

In Place of a Curse
By John Ciardi (1916-1986)

At the next vacancy for God, if I am elected,
I shall forgive last the delicately wounded who,
having been slugged no harder than anyone else,
never got up again, neither to fight back,
nor to finger their jaws in painful admiration.

They who are wholly broken, and they in whom mercy is understanding,
I shall embrace at once and lead to pillows in heaven.
But they who are the meek by trade, baiting the best of their betters with extortions
of a mock-helplessness,
I shall take last to love, and never wholly.

Let them all in Heaven - I abolish Hell -
but let it be read over them as they enter:
Beware the calculations of the meek, who gambled nothing
gave nothing, and could never receive enough.

The final element of personal responsibility is integrity. You possess nothing in life more valuable than your own good name. Fortunately our good name is something we can control. We all know how important having a good name is in business. Especially now in our wired age, your reputation is the most important thing you have. So what is your reputation? It's the accumulation of all those little actions you make every single day, which is why it's so important to make sure you are building something positive every day. That's the way we create and sustain success in our lives. Here are a couple stories to illustrate what I mean.

Story #1: During World War II, Butch O'Hare was a fighter pilot on an aircraft carrier in the Pacific. On a mission with his squadron one day, he saw he was low on fuel—someone must have forgotten to fill his fuel tank—and his leader told him to return to the ship.

On his way back, Butch saw a squadron of Japanese Zeros ready to attack the defenseless U.S. fleet (the fighter planes were all on the mission). So by himself, Butch attacked the Japanese squadron. He dove into the formation and fired until he ran out of ammunition and even then Butch kept diving, hoping to clip a wing and make the Japanese planes unfit to fly. Finally, the Japanese squadron left the area and Butch's badly shot up plane returned to the carrier.

Butch told the men on the ship what happened, but it wasn't until they watched the film of the battle—American planes were equipped with cameras to record terrain and enemy maneuvers—that Butch's incredible heroism was revealed. He was awarded the Medal of Honor, and his name became known to travelers around the world in 1947 when Chicago's O'Hare Airport was named in honor of American hero Butch O'Hare.

Story #2: In Chicago in the 1920s, there was a lawyer named Easy Eddie. He was the lawyer for the gangster Al Capone and he kept Capone out of jail during Capone's tenure as the crime boss of Chicago. Yes, Eddie was a really, really good lawyer.

Life was pretty sweet for Easy Eddie. He was the trusted lawyer and accountant to Capone and he was very well compensated for keeping the secret books and keeping the boss out of the big house. In fact, Eddie's house was so big it took up an entire Chicago block.

Eddie had a son whom he loved very much. Eddie gave his son everything he could: the most stylish clothes, the nicest car and a good education, and he tried to teach his son right from wrong. But there was one thing Eddie couldn't give his son—he couldn't pass on a good name. So Eddie decided he couldn't be Capone's lawyer anymore and agreed to testify against his boss, even though he knew it meant Capone would have him killed. Sure enough, within a year of testifying against Capone in the income tax case that put the crime boss behind bars for good, Eddie was gunned down in a hail of bullets on a lonely Chicago street.

Now I know what you're thinking: what do these stories have in common? Butch O'Hare was Easy Eddie's son.

THE LESSON

A parent with integrity sets a great example for his or her children, but if you are not living and acting morally in your own life, you won't be any help to your children when they are trying to find their way in their lives. Nothing in this world is worth trading your integrity and the example that you can show somebody for. I mean absolutely nothing in the world is worth it, not even close. I don't care how big your house is or how fast your car goes. We're going to be here a short time, and the things that you can give to people that have nothing to do with money are far more rewarding than anything you can give them in a box wrapped up with a bow. You have to be true to yourself and listen to that voice inside you because we all have it. The most important thing in work and in life is to never, ever compromise your principles.

One of my favorite hobbies is studying Civil War history, and I am always amazed at the wisdom of Abraham Lincoln and how much we still can learn from him today. The Civil War was the most challenging time our country ever faced, and in such a turbulent time, Lincoln faced plenty of criticism for his decisions, however, he never wavered from his principles. After signing the Emancipation Proclamation, Lincoln said, "I desire so to conduct the affairs of this administration that if at the end, when I come to lay down the reins of power, I have lost every other friend on earth, I shall at least have one friend left, and that friend shall be down inside me."

When you stay true to your principles, you'll never lose your most important friend of all: yourself.

CHAPTER 5

TRUE LEADERS HELP OTHERS ACHIEVE

At the beginning of this book I told you about my throwing problem during my second year in the majors and how my dad helped me face down the monster of self-doubt that was overtaking my life by admitting that he also had a throwing problem when he was in high school.

Years later, I was talking about this conversation with my mom and she said, "I have to tell you, your dad never had a throwing problem in his life." Well, my jaw just dropped. I thought, "Wait a minute. That conversation changed my life. That conversation saved my baseball career and helped me achieve my goals as a player. You mean, he really didn't have that problem?" It was like the ground I was walking on suddenly had disappeared. Then I realized that my dad had told me exactly what I needed to hear without any concern for himself and his own self-image.

That's what true leaders do. You can always tell who the good leaders are: they are the ones with the arrows in their back because they take the hits for everybody else. I believe that wholeheartedly. Leaders also know that it's not so much what they say, or even what they do, that will matter most. Instead, the important thing is how a leader makes people feel. Leaders know that sometimes people are going to forget what they say. Sometimes people are going to forget even the successes that a leader accomplishes. But when people look at a leader, they will never forget the way that leader made them feel.

And that's what my dad had done for me. I never forgot the way that he made me feel when he told me that. And I think that's true everywhere else, too. You never forget how a good leader made you feel.

If you're going to be a successful leader, you need to lead with a servant's heart. That means taking the arrows when necessary to help the entire team, and taking responsibility when things go wrong.

There could be an instance in an office where something happens—let's say the company loses an important account—and for the morale and the good of the office, the leader will step up and take responsibility for the problem. Instead of letting something negative filter out through an office, the leader will just corral the whole situation and put it on his or her desk. The leader takes responsibility for a problem so that a bad situation doesn't create even more problems as people try to assign blame.

Lots of times leaders will take the blame for things that really aren't their fault. Sometimes leaders will spread the accolades, maybe even when they're not 100 percent true. For example, I remember playing in New York, where those newspaper guys love to stir up trouble in a locker room. I don't get mad at them, that's what they get paid to do and it's something you have to deal with playing in New York.

Here's an example of how it works. Let's say there's a fly ball down the right-field line. The right fielder Jesse Barfield, the first baseman Don Mattingly and I are all converging on the baseball. And maybe nobody catches it and the ball drops, and the next thing you know the other team gets a base hit, and the Yankees lose the ball game.

So the sportswriter will come up to me after the game and say, "Looking at that play, I just talked to Jesse and Don, and they didn't say it, but they kind of questioned whether maybe you should have caught that ball." And you know what I would say? I would say, "That was not their ball. That was my ball. *I* should have caught that ball."

In truth, that ball was anybody's, but in a situation like that, the true leader takes responsibility. When I say, "There's no question about it, I should have had that ball," it shuts everything down. There is no argument, no controversy. It defuses the situation. Now it's over. Everybody makes mistakes. Nobody is perfect so, again, cut off the shackles of pressure. I'm going to make mistakes, you're going to make mistakes. The important thing isn't the mistakes you make, it's what you do to fix them and learn from them that matters most.

Now if I were to say to that sportswriter, "You know, off the record, that was Mattingly's ball," then we'd have a situation that would fester. Once you go down that route, there's no escape. Whether it's the fly ball down the line or maybe it's the FedEx package that didn't get out on time or the sales call that didn't go well, it's OK to be the big person and step up and say, "Hey, that was me." That's what leadership is about. That's what leaders do.

THE LESSON

You are the slave of what you say and the master of what you don't say. That dictum doesn't mean "never say anything." It means that you should be aware of the power of your words. There will be lots of times when you can make that beneficial to you. When I say, "That was my ball, my fault," I want people to know that I'm taking responsibility for what happened. It's similar to those conversations I would have with my friends and family when my kids were in earshot. I would talk to some of my friends and family about a certain subject, maybe it was drugs, maybe it was smoking, maybe it was drinking alcohol. And I would talk to my friends and family about the downfalls and how bad it was. Instead of preaching that message to my kids, I would talk about it with my friends and relatives so that my kids could hear it indirectly. I know they could hear it and it was going in their heads without me having to lecture them.

Another trait all effective leaders share is that they are gracious. Being gracious is probably one of the single best things that a leader can do because a leader is ultimately only as good as the people he or she leads. A true leader is thankful that he or she is working with such a great group of people. The leader is grateful for being put into a position to be able to lead—that people hold him or her in high enough esteem to ask his or her opinions. Being in a position where people look up to you is something you should appreciate, and being gracious is a huge part of being an effective leader.

How does a leader show gratitude? It's very simple. Let's say that you're at an event and you're making a public speech about the workplace and you're talking about the people on your team. You're talking about the way these people move you. You're talking about how these people make you a better leader, and that they are people who are great to work with, people whom you still learn from even though you're the leader. A good leader isn't the one saying, "Yes, I am the almighty leader. I am just the greatest." Just like a good leader on a ballclub doesn't pose for the crowd after hitting a homerun. The business leader gives credit to his team and says that without them as great teammates, leading would be a much tougher job. You just give it back to the other person. You give it back, and just are gracious for being in that leadership position. Believe me, that gratitude is going to go a long way.

One of the most gracious leaders I've ever known was Dodgers manager Tommy Lasorda. If he had to review your performance in a game and tell you some things that maybe you didn't want to hear, he certainly wouldn't do it in a packed locker room full of your colleagues. He would take you in his office and rip you a new one, but before you left his office you shook hands and it was good.

He did everything in a way that was respectful. He wouldn't talk about you in the newspapers, he wouldn't talk about you in the locker room, and he wouldn't embarrass you in front of your teammates. He would take you in his office and do what he had to do, and then everything was good afterward. That's what leaders do, and I have a lot of gratitude toward him for doing that.

The reason Tommy is in the Hall of Fame is because of the human element of what he brought to the game, the fact that he could transcend all boundaries, that he spoke different languages. He created and maintained a cohesive unit of 25 people who were from different countries and different walks of life.

The one thing that Tommy showed me was that people—no matter where they're from—really do have a lot of the same goals, and on the inside we're pretty much all the same. We want to better ourselves, and we want better things for our lives and better things for our families. Tommy was very involved with his players and their families. He really brought a personal, family touch to a business that was very regimented.

For example, let's say that you're a major league ballplayer and you're going to go out to get something to eat. One unwritten rule for teams is that if you go to an establishment to eat and the manager and coaches are there already, you have to leave. The reason is that if something happened at the restaurant—let's say a fight broke out and we were only innocent bystanders—it would be a thousand times worse if management and players were there together. Well, Tommy threw that rule out the window. Instead, he would *take* us out to eat. That's the kind of person he was. He was a very hands-on, family-type of person. What he brought to the team was a sense that we were a family unit and we had the strength and cohesion of that unit. That's why his players played so hard for him, because they respected him.

THE LESSON

A big part of leadership is doing small positive things for people that start to add up into something pretty significant. When I'm working with somebody in business, I try to give them some direction or give them an example of how they can make their business better. That's why I love working in the business that I'm in because I can put the focus on other people. When you help people develop new skills, when you start to help people out, you're really creating the next generation of leaders. That's what I really like. Showing somebody how to do something correctly, showing somebody how to carry themselves in a certain way, showing somebody how to resolve a problem in a way that somebody else will benefit from. Those are simple things that make a big difference in people's lives, and Tommy Lasorda understood that well.

It all starts with the people that you lead. Everybody that you're working with, everybody you're associated with, they all have different ways of doing things. Not right ways and wrong ways, just different ways. There's no question about it. Each person is going to be specific and unique with his or her own way of doing stuff.

Some people are going to need to be coddled. Some people are going to need to be kicked in the hind-end. And some people, you need to just get the heck out of their way. Just open the door and say, "Go!" and let them do their thing.

What that means is that a leader should not treat every person exactly the same. In fact, nobody should be treated exactly the same, because everybody's different. A good leader recognizes this and motivates each person a little bit differently.

Do the rules apply the same in the workplace? Absolutely. That's not what I'm talking about. The rules apply the same for everybody. But the way you handle people, it's all different. I've seen leaders use different motivation techniques depending on the personality of the team member, and they have gotten great results because they knew the individuals on their team and how to get the best work from them. That's what leaders are supposed to do.

You need to know what makes people tick. With every team member, ask yourself, "How do I get the most out of this person?" There are all these different ways to motivate different people and a successful leader will know what every team member needs. It's OK to motivate people in different ways. In fact, I think it's essential and the people on your team will recognize that as well. The important thing is that the same rules apply to everyone equally.

Once you know how to motivate your team, it's important to be excited for other people's accomplishments. Sure, people will get excited about making money—money is always something that spurs production. "Hey, I just got a bonus or a raise for this!" is something every worker likes to say.

But you know what's really going to get to somebody? It's when you show your gratitude toward them and you praise them in front of other people. When you let people know how great it is to work with them, I guarantee you in the long run, that praise is worth more to them than the money they just got as a bonus. When you tell somebody how much you appreciate them, that's going to go further, way further than any bonus they're going to receive.

STEVE'S TIP

I really believe that if you build the person, you're going to build the leader. You can't just install somebody in a position to take the reins or to be an example to the rest of the team until you build the person first. It starts from the inside-out. You have to build up the person. You're going to build up their self-esteem, and you're going to build up their confidence. That's what leadership is about. It's about self esteem and confidence, and showing the way for others.

When you start your day, you should think, "Somebody's going to benefit from me today." That's the essence of leadership, the essence of what we're taking about. You are a successful leader when you help other people achieve their goals. That's leading with a servant's heart. And that's why I say, "Somebody's going to benefit from me today, because I'm going to put it out there. I'm going to put out the positive energy. I'm going to put out the leadership and I am going to make whatever situation we have in front of us better." People have solutions—there are a lot of solutions out there. What we need to do is jettison the complaints and look for the solutions

Leadership is somebody who, first of all, puts others before themselves; somebody who is willing to take arrows, when they don't deserve them. I also believe that leaders are the people who aren't looking for the accolades. Instead, they spread out those accolades for other people instead of taking them all for themselves.

Leadership is an act of gratitude for others. True leaders are the ones that exemplify it, live it, and believe it. They don't just talk about leading for others. They live it every single day. It's not a script they have to follow. It's a conscience and a feeling they're following in being a leader. It's about not having a society that changes them. It's about changing their surroundings and changing society for the better by being a good leader. That's what leadership is about.

There is another element of leading by example that we sometimes overlook: our role as a leader to our children. The most important part of parenting is setting an example for your kids. If I was somebody who was out all night partying, or if my kids saw me smoking, or using bad language, then they're going to take part in those activities. They're going to think that's OK. They're not going to know the difference between me doing something as an adult and them doing it as a child. So I try to be a good example for my kids; that's the best way to lead. In fact, I think it's the only way.

Believe me, I'm far from perfect. But the thing is that nobody is perfect. Nobody is going to be a perfect example all the time. You try to do the best you can. The main thing people have to do is set examples by their own behavior and actions. Not only for your kids, but I think it's important for leaders to set a good example in the workplace. People who are leaders have got to lead by example. If they don't, no one will follow them. Lip service is something I've never admired.

THE LESSON

You'll know you're a true leader when you get excited for other people's successes. In business, we all look at numbers. We have to. Numbers are what allow us to make our payrolls and feed our families and stay in business and grow. However, you have to care about your people even more than your numbers. If people know you truly care about them, they will follow you, your production will increase, and your numbers will be better than ever.

CHAPTER 6

OVERCOMING OBSTACLES

We've come a long way so far. We've identified our why, we've created a game plan for success, we made a commitment to humility and integrity, and we've learned that the best way to lead is to help others succeed. Now I've got some good news and some bad news for you. The bad news is that you're still going to face obstacles every day, but the good news is that you can use these obstacles to strengthen your commitment to your long-term goals. As I always say, adversity has a way of introducing you to yourself. And trust me, if you're following your plan for long-term success, you're going to have some unforeseen adversity and obstacles come your way.

Have you ever heard of the C.A.V.E. people? No—not those guys who wore animal skins and carried big clubs and dragged their wives by the hair. I mean the Citizens Against Virtually Everything. Those people who just don't want to hear about anything new. "It can't work," they say. "Don't bother us," they say. "We're happy being miserable," they say.

Let's take the example of a new product or a new idea on the scene today. Remember that everything new goes through three different stages. The first stage is that people are going to say it's absolutely impossible. You'll hear the C.A.V.E. people say, "It's not going to happen." In the second stage the idea or new product is violently opposed, usually by those same C.A.V.E. people. And in the third stage the new product or idea is accepted as self-evident and those same C.A.V.E. people will forget they had ever opposed it.

When was the last time you used your microwave oven. I bet it was pretty recently. Well, the first microwave oven was built in the spring of 1947. It was 6 feet tall and weighed almost 750 pounds. It cost between

$2,000 and $3,000. The first home model was introduced in 1952 and cost $1,295. People just didn't buy microwave ovens; they were almost offended by them. They exclaimed, "That'll never work!" and "I'm not going to be poisoned by those rays zapping my food." In 1967 Tappan brought out the first countertop microwave oven and now you never see a kitchen without one. The same thing happened with cell phones and home computers. Can you imagine your life without those things today? I know I can't.

This cycle is not a new phenomenon either. Remember Copernicus from your high school science class? Born in Poland in 1473, Nicolas Copernicus was a brilliant man. He was a mathematician, a physician, a classical scholar, a translator, an artist, a cleric, a jurist, a governor, a military leader, a diplomat and an economist. Pretty busy guy, right? We remember him as an astronomer because Copernicus realized that the Earth revolved around the sun. He believed in a heliocentric cosmology, meaning that the sun is at the center of the universe and everything revolves around sun.

Back then, people thought this was crazy. They thought that this guy was an absolute nut. Everybody knew that the Earth was at the center of the universe, and the sun revolved around the earth. How could the sun be at the center if we're living on the Earth? Well, Copernicus was brash enough to say that's not the case, folks. He told those C.A.V.E. people, "I know it feels like the Earth is the immoveable center of everything, but that's not how it works."

What happened to Copernicus is the same thing that happened to microwave ovens, cell phones and computers 500 years later. If an idea or product doesn't fit the status quo of how people view the world, they will zealously oppose it. When you follow your dream in life, you are going to encounter resistance as well. You are going to hear people say, "That's impossible." They might even actively oppose you. When this happens, you need to remember that you have a dream that is important to you and stick by that dream and listen to what your heart is telling you. In our society, we've seen ideas, products and services that have been sent through the wringer before they were accepted. Those are the three stages that every new idea goes through. People are going to say it's impossible, and then they're going to be opposed to the idea because they don't want to accept it, and then pretty soon they have to accept it. Finally the idea becomes part of the new status quo. Remember that there are always going to be naysayers out there, and you just have to stick to your guns.

When something new comes out, people are going to be uncomfortable with it. When you get them outside of their comfort zone, people tend to get a bit ruffled. That's only normal. But one thing that happens in business, when you believe in something like Copernicus did, there's going to come a certain time where you're going to feel very uncomfortable about what you're doing, especially if you are working with a totally new idea or something that has never been tested.

You just have to be steadfast and go through that uncomfortable period and know that it may be a while, but that you really do owe it to yourself to go out and try to explore these new ideas. Innovation is what makes this country so unbelievably great. I see it in business today. These innovators come up with these incredible ideas and people look at them kind of crossways and say, "How do you think you're going to do that?"

If your idea is strong enough to change people's lives, then there's going to be strong opposition to it. That's probably the most uncomfortable time because you're going to hear it from your friends and family that it will never work. And then pretty soon you get some traction and things start to become self-evident. Then everything else falls into place and people will forget they ever opposed you in the first place. In fact, they'll convince themselves that they always, always believed in you, right from the very beginning.

THE LESSON

No matter how good your idea or goals are, you're going to have an uncomfortable period when people challenge you. You really can't avoid this and you just have to paw through it. When you're on the road to achieving success, people are going to doubt you. They're going to say you can't do it, and too many people listen to those doubters and let them get in their heads. Well, let me tell you once and for all, "Don't listen to the naysayers." You hear a lot of people talk about how they want to be successful. There are a lot of people who tell me that they have a goal and a plan, yet there are far fewer people who actually do it, follow through with it and make sure it happens. The reason more people don't succeed is that most people are only *wishing* for success. They're wishing for things to happen. You need more than wishes to succeed. You need to expect success and implement those successes into your everyday plans and future goals. In other words, it's time to harvest your accomplishments and put them into action.

Wishing won't get you past the C.A.V.E. people. You need something a lot stronger and sturdier than a wish. It's fine to wish for something, but you have to have a backbone not a wishbone. You've got to be tough. Part of being successful is being tough because you're going to be loaded down with naysayers.

STEVE'S TIP

Tune out the negative people in your life. It's a tough lesson to learn, but the truth is that a small number of people who are close to you don't want you to succeed. Most of the time, the naysayers are the ones who are broke.

One of my favorite stories about people who overcame the naysayers is the story of Wilma Rudolph. Wilma was born in Clarkesville, Tenn., in 1940 as one of 22 children. That's right, 22 children. Wilma was born prematurely and she caught polio as young child, which made her vulnerable to pneumonia and scarlet fever. She recovered from the illness, but she wore a brace on her left leg, which had caused her leg to grow crooked. Doctors thought she might never walk correctly again.

But Wilma's parents cared enough to take her from Clarksville to Nashville for physical therapy. A specialist in Nashville recommended massage treatment, so Wilma's mother would rub her leg numerous times every day. Wilma said later that when she was 5 years old, she spent most of her time trying to figure out how to get out of her brace and run with the other kids. Wilma finally did get out of that brace when she was 12 and she was able to run like all the other kids. Well, not exactly like the other kids. Wilma ran like the wind. She played basketball and ran track in high school, where she caught the attention of a Tennessee State track coach.

When Wilma was only 16, she earned a spot on the U.S. Olympic team at the 1956 Olympics in Melbourne, Australia, and took home a bronze medal as a member of 4 x 100 relay team. That was only a preview of what Wilma would accomplish. At the 1960 Olympics in Rome, Wilma won three gold medals and set an Olympic medal in the 200-meter dash. After the Olympics, she was known as "the fastest woman in the world." Why? Because she never quit. She never stopped. She never believed what people told her.

THE LESSON

People underestimate or won't take into account the element of passion in a human being. If you have something that you believe in, if you're with a company or in a business position where you have a good forum from which to exhibit your skills and you have passion for what you're doing and you have a game plan to go with it, I really believe that you cannot be detoured. You cannot be stopped. You won't be denied if you have those three things: a track to run on, a game plan and a lot of passion. How can you beat that?

I can't tell you how many times I've heard from the C.A.V.E. people in my life. Back when I was playing with the Dodgers, I was building a big house on the West Coast. I had lived my entire life in California, and the Dodgers never thought I would leave. But when it came time to renew my contract, the negotiations just weren't going as well as I thought they should, and the situation wasn't right for me. So what did I do? I did a pretty bold thing. I left the place where I played for 11 years and went to the New York Yankees.

It was a big change for me and my family, but at the end of the day I knew the Dodgers situation wasn't right. So what'd I do? I moved across the country and changed my situation. In life, you know when a situation isn't right. You can feel it in your heart. Say you're at your job and your boss is bearing down on the back of your neck, and he's telling you to take a lunch when he wants you to take it, and you just know this situation isn't right. You feel it in your bones. Well, you can change it. You have that power. It's up to you.

Whenever I'm in a tough situation—and I know how hard it is to walk away from something you're familiar with and go off into the great unknown—I think about something Frederick Douglass said. Do you remember learning about Frederick Douglass in school? He was born into slavery, from which he escaped as a young man, then he became an abolitionist and a great orator and he advised Abraham Lincoln when Lincoln wrote the Emancipation Proclamation. (Douglass was actually a little taller than the 6'4" President.) Douglass even wrote one of the most famous autobiographies in American literature. When they open a Hall of Fame of Overcoming Obstacles, Douglass will get his own wing.

One of the things that Douglass said holds us back is that people are willing to put up with situations they don't like. They just put up with it. And you know what? It's not going to stop until you say, "I'm done with this." It's not going to stop until you put up a stand and say, "I'm not doing this anymore. I'm going another direction." A bad situation is not going to change unless you make it change.

Douglass said, "Find out just what many people will quietly submit to and you have found out the exact measure of injustice and wrong which will be imposed upon them. And these will continue until they are resisted with either words or blows, or with both. The limits of tyrants are prescribed by the endurance of those whom they oppress."

That's the best way I've ever heard it put. "The limits of tyrants are prescribed by the endurance of those whom they oppress." What it means is that people are going to keep doing it to you, and as long as you keep doing what you're doing you're going to keep getting what you're getting...until you say, "No mas!"

I've had to make some bold changes in my life, but I made them. After my career in baseball, I worked in financial services, but at a certain point I had to get out. I wasn't comfortable with where the industry was going and it didn't feel like the right place for me anymore. So I made another huge change and now I'm happier in my work than ever before. I believe that most of the time people get exactly what they want, but you can't get what you want if you don't go after it.

I can't tell you how many times people would tell me that I was crazy. The C.A.V.E. people always say, "What do you think you're doing? I mean, do you know what the odds are for this?" And here's the thing, for average people, I believe those odds are probably correct. But if you're going to succeed you have to look at yourself as not average. Think about that: you are not average. You are someone who has committed to a game plan for success, you've planted positive things every day, you've acted with integrity and you've devoted yourself to helping others. There's nothing average about you at all, so you start looking at yourself as different from everybody else.

You also need to realize that everybody is going to go through hell in one instance or another, and you just have to drive through it. Nobody's going be exempt from tough times. We all have gone through hell at different times in our lives, and when you are there, you cannot stop and take a break. You've just got to keep on driving. You've got to keep on driving till you get through hell.

It might be a long drive, but you have got to power through it. There will be times in your life where things are just really not very good, things are the pits. That's happened to me in my life. I went through it when I got divorced. I went through it when I had my throwing problem. I knew that there were going to be periods of my life where it just wasn't going to be good, it wasn't going to be fun.

So you know what I did? I looked at the thing, and I said, "OK, this is not going to be fun for the awhile, but I can approach this in a couple of different ways. I can say, 'Poor me, I'm a victim' and I can just cower down to it and sulk around everybody and tell everybody how bad life is, or you know what I can do? I can bite it right back in the face, and that's what I did."

I choose to be positive. I choose to not be miserable and to try to make the best of whatever I can and get through this thing. That's what I've always done during difficult times in my life, just kept driving through hell.

How important is it to believe in yourself and not the averages? Let me tell you about my friend John Saca. John is one of my very dear friends. He's a big-time developer in California. About seven years ago I was with John and his wife, Darcy, at a clothes store. John and I get our clothes at the same store. I said to Darcy, "Why is John so thin? Boy, he looks really thin." Then John interrupted and said, "You know, I've been having these night sweats quite a bit lately. I've been working a lot. It's summertime. I think that's what it is."

I said, "Man, you need to go get a checkup." So he went and got a checkup, and he called me about two days later and he said, "I want to meet you for lunch." So we went out for lunch and John said, "Oh, I want to tell you something. I've been diagnosed with Stage IV-B non-Hodgkin's lymphoma."

I don't know how much you know about lymphoma, but IV-B generally means you're going to die. IV-B is like the worst of the worst that you can get. John had a tumor in his chest. He had one in his spleen. He had one in his lung. He had it all over him. This guy was gone. And there he was consoling me at lunchtime, because I was pretty broken up about this. He was the one facing this terrible disease and he was consoling me. He told me, "This is going to be a nine-month inconvenience for me. I'm going to be sick and then I'm going to be well." And deep down in my heart I was thinking, "No, you're not."

Today John has completely eradicated the cancer. Free of treatment. He has had a clear checkup for seven years now. He has completely beat it. And he's thriving. He's got two little girls, a beautiful wife and he is very happily married.

John got well because he believed it. And what I love about him is that he had a cocky smirk on his face when he told me about it at that lunch. He was so confident telling me how he was going to get better. He said, "Hey, this is a nine-month inconvenience." I said "John, you're Stage IV-B." He said, "I don't care. I'll beat this. You watch. I start my chemo and my radiation, and I will beat this. It's going to be a nine-month inconvenience."

And he did. He did it.

THE LESSON

The bottom line is that if John didn't have the mindset he did, he might very well not be here right now. That's about as blunt as I can put it. Do I believe that his mindset saved his life? There's no doubt about it. Not a question about it. What if he cowed down to this and said, "You know what? It's over. I'm Stage IV-B, I'm done"? He could have gone on Google and researched it and found out that maybe 2 percent of the people actually beat it when they're stage IV-B, but he didn't do that. John told me that this terrible disease was just a nine-month inconvenience. Why was he consoling me? He was the sick one. His attitude was astonishing. You hear great things about how people conquer certain things, but you just can't imagine the strength of the mind until you see it in action.

CHAPTER 7

CHOOSE SUCCESS

(MISERY IS OPTIONAL)

've never met a pessimist who was successful. That's kind of a broad stroke but—you know what?—I never have. I've never met somebody who always looked at the not-so-bright side or looked at the glass as half-empty or plotted to do bad things that became successful. I've never met anyone who didn't have a big dream or didn't challenge himself or herself and became successful.

I've never met somebody who was a burden to others who was successful. I never met someone who didn't have a conscience who was successful. The successful people I've known were all positive people and they weren't just out for themselves. They understood that success is about helping others.

Does success just mean that a person has a lot of money? A successful person is somebody who is happy with himself or herself. It's somebody who has built great personal relationships that have nothing to do with their work; somebody who has real strong family ties. Success is not just what you do in your vocation, but it includes all these other things that make a well-rounded person. And when you have all those things, you are a success by any definition and you'll find that money usually follows.

There's a Cherokee legend about an old Indian talking to his grandson. The old Indian says there is a terrible fight going on inside him between two wolves. One wolf is bad. His spirit is ruled by anger, jealousy, hatred and greed. This wolf stalks people, wrecks villages and does terrible things. The other wolf is good. He is full of joy, love, peace, kindness and hope. This wolf leads the other wolves in the pack and takes care of them. The grandfather tells his grandson that the same fight between those two wolves is going on inside the boy and inside every other person in the world. The young Cherokee boy is thoughtful for a minute, then asks his grandfather, "Which wolf will win?"

His grandfather says, "The one you feed."

THE LESSON

What you choose to focus your energy on is what is going to grow in your life. That's why we've talked so much about your mindset, making priorities, passion and creating something positive every day. It's not that complicated. You choose what grows inside you by what you feed it. So choose wisely.

I can tell you that there are a lot of people who control dynasties and have a ton of money that I wouldn't trade places with for anything. They don't appear to be real happy people. And that's not what I'm talking about when we say someone is successful. Sometimes when we see people who have a lot of things materially, it's really just a big façade. I've seen other people who have a ton of money, but you'd never know it. They don't try to showcase it. But I can tell you that these people are extremely successful and they certainly have a lot of money, probably a lot more money than the people who are so intent on showing you how much they have. These are the really successful people. They already know how much they've achieved—they know because they know how hard they worked for it—so they don't feel the need to show it off. These people are successful in every other part of their life as well. They've certainly achieved monetary success. They've got personal success. Family success. Personal growth. A lot of good, solid relationships in their life. Family. Friends. They've found success spiritually. There are many, many different ways of being well-rounded and successful. When you have all these important areas of your life working together in balance, I think that's what makes someone truly successful.

What prevents some people from achieving success is that too often they just accept mediocrity. Their mindset is the problem. These people don't focus on the goal of long-term success. Maybe these people are lazy or maybe they don't have ambition, hopes and dreams. Maybe they're not willing to pay the price that success demands. There are as many common denominators in unsuccessful people as there are in people who are successful. The biggest trait unsuccessful people share is that they accept mediocrity. If you accept mediocrity, then you'll never be happy with your situation at work and in life because you're not asking enough of yourself and others.

Success all starts with your mindset. Like we talked about at the beginning of this book, success starts with the positive things you build every day. With these positive acts, you keep putting pennies in the bank of success. It's all up to you. Misery is only an option. What you choose to think of the most will grow the most, so don't choose misery, because it will only grow. I'm not going to get up in the morning and say, "Oh gosh, I've got to go to work today." You know, if you feel that way, like you're dreading what you have to do every day, change it. If you don't like the way our country's going and if you want to have an opinion about the way our country is run, go out and vote. If you want to do something different in your life, why don't you do something about it? Go and take a look in the mirror. Right there you'll find 99 percent of all your answers. You're looking right at the answer. It's you. So do something about it. People get mostly what they want. So if there's something you want to change in your life, make a bold step and do it. Don't wait for life to come to you.

STEVE'S TIP

I've got a secret about creating something positive every day. It's pretty easy to do. A lot of people choose misery because they think that's the easy way and they get lots of sympathy and attention, but if you have a laugh or you start to smile your body releases a certain kind of endorphin that actually makes you feel good. It lowers your blood pressure too. It's much healthier for you to laugh, smile and be positive than be miserable. That's why happy people tend to live longer than unhappy people. If you want to be miserable, you have every opportunity to do it, but it takes about the same amount of effort to be miserable as it does to be positive and cheerful. It takes about the same amount of energy to do either one. You just choose what side you want to go to. You pick your mindset.

Personally, I will never choose to be miserable because being a positive person creates so much energy and adds so much joy to your life. A professional singer on average makes a mistake in a live performance at least twice per song, but the singer has the ability to turn a stumble into a pirouette. Positive momentum allows you to turn a negative into a positive in the same way that a poet turns a phrase.

I'm not advising you to be mindlessly happy all the time like a Muppet. You're going to have ups and downs in business and in life. The path to success is not vertical. It doesn't go straight up. You're going to have some down times when obstacles and adversity trip you up. That's what *Shift: Change Your Mindset and You Change Your World* is all about. It's about staying focused on your long-term goals and creating something positive every day, because in the short term you're going to have times when things are difficult and you need that positive momentum you've created to carry you through.

I think a trap people can fall into is that they get too emotional on their way to success. What would be a big advantage for people is to try to not become so emotionally attached. And it's a fine line to walk because what we do in our lives is what we love and that is certainly going to breed a lot of emotion. There's no question about that. But what's important is that you can at times put a mathematical type of attitude into your business, or put a mathematical way of thinking into achieving your goals. You're going to be better off this way because that rational mindset will keep you from getting bitten by the emotional bug too much.

People who are overly dramatic, people who have all this drama in their lives, they're really just looking for attention. In the same way that we don't lose our minds over every little uptick and dip in the stock market, you need to stay balanced in your life as you work toward achieving your goals. One of the best examples of how people get too dramatic with their lives is the use of the word "awesome."

The Battle of Manassas or the Battle of the Wilderness in the Civil War, those were probably pretty awesome things. When the space shuttle takes off, that's a pretty awesome sight. But if someone in your office is wearing a new suit, and somebody says, "Man, that suit is awesome," well, that suit is not awesome. It's just a nice suit.

The speech that Abraham Lincoln delivered at Gettysburg, that was awesome. When Martin Luther King said, "I have a dream," that was awesome. But getting a new car with leather seats is not awesome. It's just a nice car.

THE LESSON

Don't mistake sensationalism for enthusiasm. Too many times people over-dramatize things. You've got to eliminate the drama and accentuate the positive so that when there's a little downturn or setback, you don't overact. You need to have perspective so that every little mishap isn't the end of the world and every minor achievement isn't the greatest thing ever. Not everything is "OMG!"

Now, I'm not saying you won't have emotional highs as you follow your game plan to success. You will and they are exhilarating. It can be a great ride for you, and sometimes these emotional highs can be really important to give you a burst of energy and help you blast through stressful times. But, if you look at the big picture, you can't just ride a wave forever. If you're riding a high, there is going to be a time when you have to come down. That's just the way life is.

If you smooth out those highs and lows, you'll have a little bit of an easier ride in life. Sure, there will be times and periods and pockets in your life where being on that emotional high is so important. For me, the playoffs and the World Series, that's a finite amount of time. It's a short time in your life where, man, it's really important to just be in an all-time high. That's what it did for me. It was great.

When it was over, I can remember being in the locker room after we beat the Oakland As in 1988. I sat down, I took my uniform off and

I put it in a bag for posterity. I wanted to keep it. Everything was going on around me in the next room. I could hear the champagne popping, screams and cameras and just a gush of people, but if I had a pillow I could have gone to sleep in a chair in that room.

That's how mentally exhausted I was. Of course, about two or three days after the game I got the flu real bad, and I was sick for about a week. Everybody on my team did too. It wasn't because somebody caught a bug somewhere. It was because you let your senses down, your defenses down and finally it was all over, and when you finally let your defenses down, you're going to get sick.

THE LESSON

It's good to have that emotional high for some periods of time. The emotional high got me and my teammates through the World Series, but there's always going to be a price to pay somewhere else. Use the emotional highs when you have to, but you need balance to sustain you on the road to long-term success.

Let's say that a waitress is going through a restaurant. She's got her pot of coffee and she's going over and she's asking people, "Would you like coffee?" We've seen this happen a hundred times at our favorite diner. She'll go from table to table, and she'll say "Coffee?" And they'll say, "No." She'll go to the next table. "Coffee?" "No." "Coffee?" "No." "Coffee?" "No." "Coffee?" "Yes." Ah, somebody said, "Yes." So she pours them the coffee.

But the waitress did not get upset at the six people she asked before that person said yes to the coffee—the six people who said, "No, I don't want the coffee." She didn't get upset that they said no to her. She didn't get emotional. She was just going about her job. Just because they said no to the coffee, they weren't saying no to her. They were saying no to the coffee. So she doesn't get upset about it.

Now let me give you another example. Let's say that you're a real estate agent, and you're going to make the sale for a house. And a buyer comes up to you and he is just loaded with excitement. "Oh my gosh! It's the most perfect house! It's a four-bedroom! We've got two kids. It's absolutely perfect! It's in a great school district! This is absolutely perfect—and we would love to buy this house from anybody but you." Now if somebody says that, OK, then you've got a problem. But 99.99 percent of the time, when somebody says, "No," they're saying it to the coffee, not you. If you think like that waitress, you'll realize how silly it is to get worked up over a "No," and you'll be able to stay positive until somebody says, "Yes." Because they will.

If you follow these steps for lasting success, I know you will achieve your goals, because when you have a dream, a game plan, drive, a positive attitude and a focus on serving others not yourself, you'll always win. Just wake up every day and say, "This is it, somebody is going to benefit from me today." What you give to others will come back to you tenfold. Stick to your principles and similar people will find you.

Remember, you already have every basic element to do something really, really great in your life. The only limitations we have are the ones we create for ourselves. We live in a country that allows us to do so many great things and to be innovative and free-thinking. The sky is the limit. Never underestimate the power and will of the human spirit.

Steve Sax had a successful baseball career with the Los Angeles Dodgers, the New York Yankees, the Chicago White Sox, and the Oakland Athletics. He won two World Series rings, was the 1982 National League Rookie of the Year, and made five all-star teams. In 2001, realizing that he had accomplished his professional baseball aspiration; he rededicated his talents to helping individuals and families to manage their finances as Vice President of Investments for the Royal Bank of Canada. Steve holds a high position with ACN, the world's largest direct seller of telecom and home services. He is an active motivational speaker on the topics of leadership, motivation, team building and personal development. Steve has two children, Lauren and John.

To learn more about Steve and for booking inquiries, please visit:

www.stevesaxspeaks.com

To learn more about ACN, please visit:

www.stephenlsax.acnrep.com

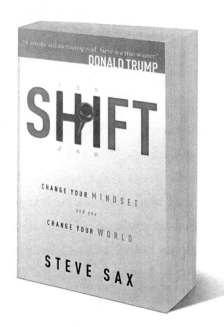

How can you use this book?

MOTIVATE

EDUCATE

THANK

INSPIRE

PROMOTE

CONNECT

Why have a custom version of *Shift*?

- Build personal bonds with customers, prospects, employees, donors, and key constituencies

- Develop a long-lasting reminder of your event, milestone, or celebration

- Provide a keepsake that inspires change in behavior and change in lives

- Deliver the ultimate "thank you" gift that remains on coffee tables and bookshelves

- Generate the "wow" factor

Books are thoughtful gifts that provide a genuine sentiment that other promotional items cannot express. They promote employee discussions and interaction, reinforce an event's meaning or location, and they make a lasting impression. Use your book to say "Thank You" and show people that you care.

Shift is available in bulk quantities and in customized versions at special discounts for corporate, institutional, and educational purposes. To learn more please contact our Special Sales team at:

1.866.775.1696 • sales@advantageww.com • www.AdvantageSpecialSales.com

Breinigsville, PA USA
03 December 2010
250587BV00004B/3/P